Second Editi

Team Building Through Physical Challenges

A Complete Toolkit

Leigh Anderson

Daniel W. Midura

Donald R. Glover

HUMAN
KINETICS

Library of Congress Cataloging-in-Publication Data

Names: Anderson, Leigh Ann, 1969- author. | Midura, Daniel W., 1948- author. | Glover, Donald R., author.

Title: Team building through physical challenges : a complete toolkit / Leigh Anderson, Daniel W. Midura, Donald R. Glover.

Description: Second Edition. | Champaign, Illinois : Human Kinetics, [2020] | Previous edition: 1992.

Identifiers: LCCN 2019008354 (print) | LCCN 2019010576 (ebook) | ISBN 9781492592785 (epub) | ISBN 9781492566939 (PDF) | ISBN 9781492566922 (print)

Subjects: LCSH: Teamwork (Sports) | Physical education and training--Study and teaching.

Classification: LCC GV706.8 (ebook) | LCC GV706.8 .G58 2020 (print) | DDC 796.01--dc23

LC record available at https://lccn.loc.gov/2019008354

ISBN: 978-1-4925-6692-2 (print)

This book is a revised edition of *Essentials of Team Building,* published in 2005 by Human Kinetics, Inc. and *Building Character, Community, and a Growth Mindset in Physical Education,* published in 2017 by Human Kinetics, Inc.

The web addresses cited in this text were current as of May 2019, unless otherwise noted.

Safety Reminder: The reasonable risks present in the challenges and activities in this book could result in physical harm, but can be minimized by following the safety suggestions in chapter 4 and the specific instructions for each activity. The authors and publisher do not assume responsibility for the use of information offered in this book either written or implied.

Acquisitions Editor: Scott Wikgren; **Developmental Editor:** Jacqueline Eaton Blakley; **Managing Editors:** Anna Lan Seaman and Julia R. Smith; **Copyeditor:** Laura Stoffel; **Permissions Manager:** Dalene Reeder; **Graphic Designer:** Denise Lowry; **Cover Designer:** Keri Evans; **Cover Design Associate:** Susan Rothermel Allen; **Photograph (cover):** © Human Kinetics; **Photographs (interior):** © Human Kinetics, unless otherwise noted; **Photo Asset Manager:** Laura Fitch; **Photo Production Manager:** Jason Allen; **Senior Art Manager:** Kelly Hendren; **Illustrations:** © Human Kinetics, unless otherwise noted; **Printer:** Data Reproductions Corporation

We thank Roseville Area Schools in Minnesota for assistance in providing the location of Falcon Heights Elementary School for the photo shoot for this book. We also thank Gopher Sport for providing images for this book. Contact: Gopher, P.O. Box 998, Owatonna, MN 55060 (phone number 800-533-0446)

The video contents of this product are licensed for private home use and traditional, face-to-face classroom instruction only. For public performance licensing, please contact a sales representative at **www.HumanKinetics.com/SalesRepresentatives**.

Printed in the United States of America   10 9 8 7 6 5 4 3 2 1

The paper in this book is certified under a sustainable forestry program.

Human Kinetics
P.O. Box 5076
Champaign, IL 61825-5076
Website: www.HumanKinetics.com

In the United States, email info@hkusa.com or call 800-747-4457.
In Canada, email info@hkcanada.com.
In the United Kingdom/Europe, email hk@hkeurope.com.

For information about Human Kinetics' coverage in other areas of the world,
please visit our website: **www.HumanKinetics.com**

E7302

Tell us what you think!
Human Kinetics would love to hear what we
can do to improve the customer experience.
Use this QR code to take our brief survey.

To Sam, Jake, Josh, Lily, Annika, Jayden, and Jack. Watching you all grow into such fine young men and women has been a joy and a privilege. I can't wait to see what the future holds for each of you. Remember: Teamwork makes the dream work.

To my coauthors, Dan and Don. Thank you for allowing me to be a part of your team in writing this book. I can't imagine two better teammates.

—Leigh Anderson

To my wife, Shirley, for her incredible role as my caregiver during the past four years of my cancer journey.

To my oncology team and nursing staff at the University of Minnesota Cancer Center for serving us during countless procedures, surgeries, and treatments.

To our grandchildren, Isaiah, Eliza, and Cameron, I hope I am blessed to live long enough to see you participate in the activities we have created.

—Dan Midura

To my wife, Carol. It was an honor and privilege to be married to her for 53 years.

—Don Glover

CONTENTS

PART I   Facilitating the Team-Building Process

CHAPTER 1   Introduction to Team Building   3

CHAPTER 2   Setting Teams Up for Success   11

CHAPTER 7   Intermediate Challenges   115

CHAPTER 8   Advanced Challenges   173

PREFACE

Teamwork is a key factor in the overall success of any team or organization. In comparing the philosophies of the winningest coaches and the most successful leaders in the business world, team chemistry is often at the top of the list when it comes to achieving success. Team chemistry doesn't just happen, however. Trust among team members doesn't magically appear once individuals are placed on a team. For teams to achieve optimal performance, the necessary skills need to be taught and practiced. *Team Building Through Physical Challenges, Second Edition,* provides more than 60 activities and challenges that build these skills in fun, challenging, and engaging ways.

Team building is a cooperative process that a group of individuals uses to solve both physical and mental challenges. It's ideal for physical education, sports and recreational settings, the classroom, and the workplace. The following skills and concepts are facilitated:

- Trust building
- Conflict resolution
- Leadership
- Self-control
- Collaborative problem solving
- Effective communication
- Critical thinking
- Creativity
- Optimistic thinking
- Listening skills
- Appropriate risk taking
- Resilience
- Growth mindset

We have learned firsthand the value of team building during the nearly 40 years since we first started using what we then called *group tasks* or *problem-solving activities*. Way back then, we recognized that many activities in physical education required teamwork, yet teaching teamwork wasn't a priority. Arguing, blaming, and put-downs often occurred among teammates, especially when things got tough. We saw this as an excellent learning opportunity, especially because teamwork is such a key factor in lifelong success.

In just the past couple decades, we've witnessed the excitement and success enjoyed by thousands of people who have attended our classes and workshops. We've seen transformations occur among students, athletic teams, doctors and nurses, and business associates. It's pretty exciting to witness what happens when leaders purposefully teach respectful competition, teamwork, selflessness, and positive character development through team building.

In addition to seven new activities, as well as all the information you need to start using team-building challenges, this book is a sort of "greatest hits" collection that includes many of the best activities we've used for years and have shared in various books we've published:

- *Team Building Through Physical Challenges*
- *More Team Building Challenges*
- *Character Education*
- *Essentials of Team Building*
- *Building Character, Community, and a Growth Mindset in Physical Education*

Also new in this book is guidance for teaching the skills necessary to develop and maintain a growth mindset. Whether it be education, athletics, or the professional world, the challenges associated with learning and growth are often overlooked. We want our climate and culture to be safe, but growth inevitably includes obstacles, frustration, and even changing behaviors, all of which can lead to discomfort. As leaders, we sometimes protect our students from discomfort when, in reality, discomfort is often where the magic happens. It's important to help students recognize that failure and obstacles often provide the best learning opportunities. In team building, failure is inevitable. By learning how to be critical thinkers and problem solvers, teams will grow closer and stronger as they learn how to positively navigate through adversity together.

Goal setting is an added component to *Team Building Through Physical Challenges, Second Edition*. Goal setting can be a highly effective strategy in helping teams maximize performance if done correctly. Goals must be followed through and reflected upon on a regular basis. All too often after goals are set, they are left alone. Teachers and coaches have the best intentions when they encourage teams to set goals, but then the "full speed ahead" mentality kicks in. The power in slowing down and going deeper is often not understood or viewed as a priority. The GROWTH goal-setting guide provided in this book places the emphasis on the behaviors needed to reach goals, not just set goals.

Character education, reflection, and assessment are explored and integrated into team-building concepts. Participants will engage in self-evaluation, allowing them to better understand how they function as a teammate and how they work through frustration. Participants will recognize that success and failure are a direct result of how individuals function as a team. Will team members blame, give up, or make excuses in difficult times, or will they problem solve, encourage each other, and positively overcome their challenges? By learning how to praise and encourage teammates and maintain a growth mindset, team bonds will be strengthened. Teams will learn to recognize that the gift often lies in the struggle and the feeling of success is that much sweeter when the challenge is eventually accomplished.

In this book, we provide you with both the principles and practices of effective team building.

- Chapter 1 details the purpose of team building and lays the groundwork for the rest of the book. Concepts such as social-emotional learning, growth mindset, critical thinking, leadership, and emotional intelligence are addressed.

- Chapter 2 focuses on how to facilitate the character traits necessary to become resilient, supportive teammates.

- Chapter 3, discusses some of the best teaching and learning tools: reflection and assessment.

- Chapter 4 describes safety considerations and equipment needed to promote a positive team-building atmosphere and minimize the risk factors of these activities.

- Chapters 5 through 8 includes a collection of our all-time best team activities and challenges along with several new ones, some of which can be conducted outdoors. The necessary components needed to facilitate these activities are listed, such as setup, rules, equipment needed, and variations.

With the purchase of this book, you also gain access to a web resource full of material to help you lead groups in these activities and challenges:

- Assessments, handouts, and other teaching tools referred to in the book
- A complete team-building course outline with 36 daily lessons
- Challenge cards and organizer cards for most of the challenges in the book

Team building is an excellent way to facilitate the skills necessary to achieve goals, win championships, and build college and career readiness skills. No matter what the setting, productivity, progress, and achievement will increase when participants truly grasp that individuals working together toward a common goal far outperform individuals working in isolation. We tend to agree with MLB baseball legend Babe Ruth when he stated, "The way a team plays as a whole determines its success. You may have the greatest bunch of individual stars in the world, but if they don't play together, the club won't be worth a dime" (www.baberuth.com/quotes).

HOW TO USE THE WEB RESOURCE

Team Building Through Physical Challenges, Second Edition, includes access to a web resource that will assist you in leading teams through the team-building challenges in the book. Follow the instructions on the keycode letter in the front of the book to access your material.

On the web resource you will find all of the following:

• **Video demonstrations.** When you read the challenges in the book, it might be hard to envision exactly how they will play out with your group. After all, the challenges are meant to be open ended, to set up a problem that teams can solve in more than one way. With these video demonstrations, you can see for yourself how a group of students goes about solving selected challenges. As authors Daniel W. Midura and Donald R. Glover lead students through the problem-solving process, you also see masterful demonstration of how to facilitate your team as they tackle problems and work together. See page xiv for a list of the challenges demonstrated; in addition, challenges in the book that are demonstrated on the web resource include a video icon.

• **Challenge cards and organizer cards.** Each challenge requires the use of a challenge card and organizer card designed for that specific activity. On the web resource you can access cards for most of the challenges and download them for use in an electronic device or print them out.

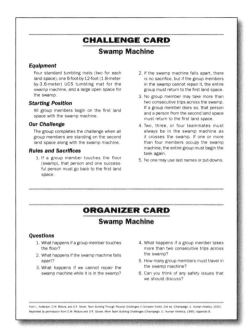

- **Reproducible forms.** The book refers to many assessments, worksheets, and other forms that will assist you in proactively teaching your team members the necessary skills to become great teammates. On the web resource you can download and print any of these forms for your team. Forms available on the web resource are marked with a WR icon in the book.

- **Course outline.** A 12-week team-building course outline is featured on the web resource. This outline walks you through plans for 36 classes to lead your team in developing teamwork skills.

VIDEO MENU

Acknowledgments

Thanks to Kathy Bergman and Ellen Fahey for reviewing this manuscript. We have a tremendous amount of respect for Ellen and Kathy and appreciate their time, knowledge, and wisdom.

Paul Shirilla, PhD, department chairmen and outdoor education professor at the University of Wisconsin at River Falls, incorporated several popular outdoor activities into team-building challenges. Great ideas were also provided by Victoria A. Otto, who was 2011 Secondary PE Teacher of the Year for the Illinois Association for Health, Physical Education, Recreation and Dance and 2012 Secondary PE Teacher of the Year for the SHAPE Midwest district.

PART I

FACILITATING THE TEAM-BUILDING PROCESS

Chapter 1

Introduction to Team Building

Team building is a cooperative process that a group of individuals uses to solve both physical and mental challenges. In working together, individuals develop character assets and interpersonal skills that prepare them for a lifetime of positive interactions in work and life. Collaboration, leadership, critical thinking, resilience, and creativity are a few of the many qualities that define success in the real world and are strengthened in fun and challenging ways through team building.

Today, countless studies demonstrate the positive effects teamwork has on productivity, motivation, and success. But what constitutes a team, and how do individuals know how to be good teammates? Individuals do not magically become supportive, trustworthy teammates when placed on a team. Individuals must be intentionally taught *how* to be supportive, trustworthy teammates to learn all the rich lessons afforded by team-building challenges.

Team building is valuable in any setting where a group of people are expected to work together toward a common goal. Physical education classes, the general education classroom, and sports and recreational settings are natural starting points for team building, but the activities and challenges presented in this book are applicable to any setting where teamwork is necessary.

Research overwhelmingly supports the importance of team building and indicates that success among teams and organizations increases when team members look beyond themselves and work toward a common goal. Trust is a crucial factor in successful teams, and leaders must facilitate this trust by strengthening connections among their teammates. Team building through physical challenges is a fun, engaging, and effective way to facilitate the skills necessary to become trustworthy, resilient teammates. A 2016 *Forbes* article, "Why Team Building Is the Most Important Investment You'll Make," noted that team building "builds trust, mitigates conflict, encourages communication, and increases collaboration. Effective team building means more engaged employees, which is good for company culture and boosting the bottom line. It can also be adventurous and enjoyable if you do it with a little pizzazz."

Physical challenges provide the "pizzazz" of team building as they get participants up and moving and thinking outside the box. Having fun together, struggling together, and succeeding together can build relationships in powerful ways. Adversity is part of every challenge, which is an added benefit. For trust and growth to occur, teammates have to confront and explore questions such as these: Will my teammates be there for me if I make a mistake, or will they put me down or blame me? Will setbacks divide us, or will they make us stronger? Leaders must be upfront about the difficulties teammates will face when working through team-building challenges and provide the tools necessary for participants to learn how to be supportive teammates who build each other up and work collaboratively through setbacks. In team building through physical challenges, participants will learn that adversity often provides the best opportunity for growth. Instead of reacting with blame or excuses, or giving up when frustration sets in, participants will embrace adversity for what it is: an opportunity to learn and grow stronger together.

Emotional Intelligence and Social-Emotional Learning

Emotional intelligence and adversity are closely linked because how a person reacts to setbacks depends on how emotionally intelligent he or she is. Team-building challenges help individuals develop and strengthen their emotional intelligence, which can be defined as the way people react to their own emotions and the emotions of others. Emotions are tested most in stressful situations. Powerful emotions can lead to poor judgment; eye rolling, blaming others, quitting, or saying or doing something inappropriate or hurtful are often the go-to behaviors. Emotionally intelligent people are skilled at managing their emotions and controlling impulses toward aggressive actions when provoked by strong emotions such as anger or frustration. Teaching students that frustration is a common feeling and that it's okay to feel this way is important. Team building provides a proactive and engaging approach for developing self-control when frustration sets in. Participants learn self-control by recognizing how negative emotions can result in negative reactions and then brainstorming and practicing positive alternatives. Teams *will* fail when attempting the physical challenges, and frustration *will* occur. Participants need to think carefully about whether their reactions toward failed attempts will help the team or hurt the team. Positive behaviors in response to negative emotions must be taught, practiced, and reinforced. By doing so, emotional intelligence will be strengthened.

It's critical to proactively teach students the social-emotional skills necessary to respond in a positive manner to stress and frustration.

In addition to learning how to manage their own emotions, participants in team building also learn how to positively influence the emotions of others. Participants are taught how to effectively praise others when the opportunity arises and, perhaps more importantly, how to encourage others when things aren't going well. Teaching techniques for praise and encouragement provides the tools necessary to think more optimistically. Additionally, valuable leadership and communication skills are being addressed as participants learn how to build up and motivate their teammates. Chapter 2 includes activities that facilitate stronger emotional intelligence.

Growth Mindset

The distinction between a growth mindset and a fixed mindset is commonly explored in education, in the business world, and on athletic teams to help individuals and teams positively work through failure and frustration. In Carol Dweck's book *Mindset: The New Psychology of Success* (2007), she states that people with a growth mindset "believe their most basic abilities can be developed through dedication and hard work—brains and talent are just the starting point. This creates a love of learning and a resilience that is essential for great accomplishment." Individuals with a growth mindset recognize that failure provides valuable opportunities to learn and improve. In contrast, people with a fixed mindset tend to fear failure and shy away from challenges; they give up more easily and make excuses or quit when setbacks occur. By developing a growth mindset, people recognize and embrace the challenges that contribute to growth, learning, and—ultimately—success. They are more resilient and more likely to take risks.

In team building, it's all about the journey toward accomplishing a challenge, and failure is acknowledged as an inevitable part of that journey. Teammates' natural behaviors in tough times are negative actions in response to negative emotions. When teamwork is properly facilitated, however, leaders set teams up for success by teaching participants how to manage emotions and recognize failure as a stepping stone toward growth. By proactively teaching a growth mindset, leaders facilitate the skills needed not only to succeed in physical challenges but also to succeed in life. Chapter 2 provides engaging activities to teach a growth mindset.

Leadership Skills

Strong leaders often have well-developed emotional intelligence and a growth mindset, which are reinforced by team building. Strong teams recognize that each person is a valued member of the team. Often the smartest or most athletic students are assumed to have the most value; in team building, however, different skill sets are needed to succeed in the challenges, and all participants have the opportunity to evolve into a leadership role. Leadership happens in many different ways; "leading by example" or "leading from behind" are two phrases often used to describe effective leaders. A leader's main objective should be to positively influence the direction of a team. Leadership is demonstrated in team building when participants have the opportunity to do the following:

- Clearly express opinions or ideas
- Respectfully listen to the ideas of others
- Recognize the strengths of each member and help match those strengths with various tasks
- Demonstrate calm behavior and encourage others when frustration or adversity occurs
- Praise the positive efforts and behaviors of team members
- Encourage teammates in challenging situations and times of adversity
- Foster group trust and communication
- Demonstrate a growth mindset through words and actions

It's fun to see the most reserved participants evolve into leaders. Participants who persevere or maintain positive attitudes and encourage others will quickly realize their impact and feel a sense of significance, no matter how athletic or unathletic they are. Assigned roles such as organizer, praiser, and encourager provide leadership opportunities in subtle, nonthreatening ways. Chapter 2 explains each role in detail and shows how to set students up for success in each of the roles.

Team building offers a variety of leadership opportunities for all team members.

College and Career Readiness Skills

Problem solving, communication skills, and critical thinking are key factors in college and career readiness. Fortune 500 companies list these in the top 10 most desirable character traits for employees. Teaching and encouraging students to be creative in their thinking will allow them to be better problem solvers. To succeed in the team-building challenges, participants must learn how to communicate and brainstorm creative solutions. After failed attempts, teams will soon realize that they need to take a step back, analyze the situation, reflect on what went well and what went wrong, and generate possible solutions. By learning to think outside the box, participants develop creativity and persistence that will reward them in all areas of life, including on the court, in the classroom, or in the workplace. Learning how to positively communicate is a natural byproduct of team building. In addition to learning to support each other when setbacks occur, teammates will learn how to become better listeners, which is essential for strong communication skills.

Building a Safe Community

Imagine an environment in which all participants felt significant and cared for, regardless of their ability, appearance, or socioeconomic status. Purposefully teaching individuals how to trust, accept, and care for each other builds a community of learners who feel connected and safe, both physically and emotionally. This sense of safety, in turn, allows students to take risks and trust those around them. In Donna Walker Tileston's book, *Ten Best Teaching Practices: How Brain Research, Learning Styles, and Standards Define Teaching Competencies* (2011), she writes the following:

> If we cannot create a climate in which students feel physically and emotionally secure, the rest doesn't matter. All of us want to belong somewhere. We want to feel we are part of the experience and that we are accepted. When students do not feel accepted, for whatever reason, they are more likely to find negative places to belong. This lack of acceptance is what helps keeps gangs alive in our students' lives. Gangs and other negative influences fill a need that so often is not met in positive settings. As educators we must create an environment in which students feel safe and accepted, an environment in which we are all learners together and where we feel a sense of togetherness. (p. 13)

A sense of belonging and significance are essential needs that drive motivation and behavior. Being a valued member of a team provides that sense of belonging and significance. The best leaders recognize and build on the strengths of all participants and send a message that everyone has a purpose and the ability to contribute. In addition, teaching students how to recognize the strengths in others and to celebrate individual differences will make them less likely to discriminate or develop entitled feelings. As a result, team building provides an excellent, proactive antidote to bullying.

The terms *character education, emotional intelligence, community building,* and *social justice* have common themes, such as compassion, empathy, respect, and acceptance. Schools and youth teams are microcosms of a much larger and very diverse world. Nelson Mandela (2003) once said, "Education is the most powerful weapon we can use to change the world." Leaders need to recognize the impact they have on the many young lives they influence every day. Teaching participants how to be supportive teammates through team building equips them with the necessary skills to embrace diversity and be positive contributors toward a more socially just world.

Adventure Education and Team Building

We often get asked about the link between adventure education and team building. The challenges, objectives, and benefits are very similar. The main difference is that adventure education typically takes place in the outdoors in natural settings. The challenges involved with team building can take place both indoors and outdoors; they are mobile and can be transferred to different settings.

Summary

Whether the objectives of your program are to develop trust, strengthen relationships, facilitate a growth mindset, teach self-control, create leaders, build college and career readiness skills, or prevent bullying, team building is one of the most effective ways to do so. The performance of both individuals and teams will be maximized when team-building skills that create trustworthy teammates and resilient teams are facilitated and then practiced in engaging, meaningful ways. Team building through physical challenges, with the proper foundational skills, is an essential component in any situation where teamwork or community building is practiced.

References

Dweck, C. 2007. *Mindset: The New Psychology of Success,* Updated ed. (New York City: Ballantine Books).

Mandela, N. 2003. "Lighting Your Way to a Better Future." http://db.nelsonmandela.org/speeches/pub_view.asp?pg=item&ItemID=NMS909&txtstr=education%20is%20the%20most%20powerful.

Scudamore, B. 2016. "Why Team Building is the Most Important Investment You'll Make." www.forbes.com/sites/brianscudamore/2016/03/09/why-team-building-is-the-most-important-investment-youll-make/#2779c392617f.

Walker Tileston, D. 2011. *Ten Best Teaching Practices: How Brain Research, Learning Styles, and Standards Define Teaching Competencies,* 3rd ed. (Thousand Oaks, CA: Corwin).

Chapter 2

Setting Teams Up for Success

Having teams attempt the physical challenges presented in this book without proactively exploring the concepts of teamwork, failure, growth mindset, and problem solving will likely result in negative experiences and conflict. People do not automatically become excellent teammates when they are placed on a team; instead, teaching teamwork skills is a critical step in facilitating positive and meaningful team interactions. This chapter is about setting participants up for success and includes several activities that will help a leader teach the qualities necessary to be optimistic, supportive teammates who form resilient, unified teams.

Specifically, this chapter includes the following concepts:

- The importance of proactively setting teams up for success
- The purpose and importance of using Y-charts
- The connection between the physical challenges and a growth mindset
- Teaching praise and encouragement
- Strengthening emotional intelligence through encouragement
- Reflection
- Student leadership roles
- Facilitating the challenges

Facilitating Social-Emotional Skills Through Y-Charts

Y-charts are an excellent strategy to teach the social-emotional and conflict-resolution skills. Through the Y-chart approach, students are encouraged use prior knowledge to construct their own meaning and strengthen their understanding of the concept being taught. To use this strategy, a teacher posts a Y-chart, which is really just a big letter Y; circle the Y to create a pie chart split into three segments: feels like, sounds like, looks like (see figure 2.1). This visual then guides a discussion as students explore a concept by considering what it feels like, sounds like, and looks like. While the students share their responses for each category, the teacher records them on a Y-chart. In these discussions, ownership is on the students; they are doing the thinking and, therefore, the learning. When participants are involved in their learning, motivation increases.

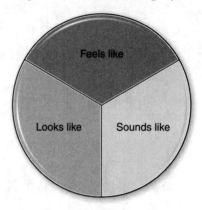

Figure 2.1 Y-chart.

Discussing the concept of teamwork is a great place to begin. Divide the group into small groups of two to four members; begin in small groups because students may not yet fully understand how to be a good teammate. Assign each small group a piece of the Y-chart. Each group brainstorms only its assigned portion of the chart—either what teamwork looks like, sounds like, or feels like. The class will probably include eight or nine groups, so each portion of the chart will be addressed by more than one group. Give the groups three to five minutes to answer their question and then have them report their reflections to the whole group. Write the responses on a Y-chart displayed on chart paper, and hang the finished chart in the room to serve as a constant reminder of what teamwork looks like, sounds like, and feels like.

Another strategy would be to give each small group the opportunity to fill in all three portions of the chart. When the small groups share with the whole group, their ideas are recorded on a larger chart to be hung in the gym or classroom.

To encourage movement, have small groups walk as they brainstorm thoughts about their portion of the Y-chart.

- Teamwork *looks like* people close together, wearing uniforms of the same color, giving and receiving high fives, and working and having fun together.
- Teamwork *sounds like* phrases such as "nice pass" and hand slaps from high fives.
- Teamwork *feels like* a sense of belonging, being comfortable, and experiencing happiness.

Y-charts are also a proactive way to solve problems. For example, the common task of having students pick partners inevitably ends up in conflict or hurt feelings. If you say, "Explain some potential problems that come with picking partners," students almost always respond with one of the following reasons:

- People will only choose their friends.
- People will be left out.

Now that potential problems have been identified, let students brainstorm possible solutions.

Ask the students, "If we want to pick partners and avoid the conflicts listed, what would choosing partners look like, sound like, and feel like?"

Brainstorming

To continue to set teams up for success, ask participants to brainstorm the traits that make a good teammate. As students construct and then further explore the qualities of a good teammate, they will better understand how to act when working with their teammates on challenges. Start the discussion by saying, "You've learned what teamwork looks like, sounds like, and feels like. Today you have the opportunity to practice what you've learned by working in teams of three of four. In your teams, list at least five character traits of a supportive team member."

After teams have finished brainstorming, allow two or three minutes for students to share their responses with the whole group. Consider completing a character trait mind map (see figure 2.2) as responses are shared. The completed posters can be placed on the walls to serve as constant reminders. When asked the qualities of a good teammate, participants may respond with one of the following qualities:

- Supportive
- Good listener
- Respectful
- Friendly

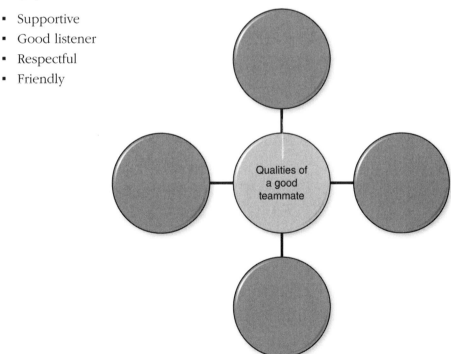

Figure 2.2 Mind map for breaking down qualities that make a good teammate.

Use the traits the students listed to further break down these concepts using a Y-chart. Ask the students, "Yes, good teammates are respectful, but what does respect look like, sound like, and feel like?" Focus on one word a week or a month to facilitate understanding of these powerful character traits. Listening is a good word to start with; tell the students, "With a partner, take a three-minute walk and talk about what listening sounds like, looks like, and feels like."

Reflection

Reflection is a valuable tool to help students think about what kind of teammate they are and what kind of teammate they hope to be. Writing responses to the following questions will help students internalize how their words and actions impact those around them (see figure 2.3):

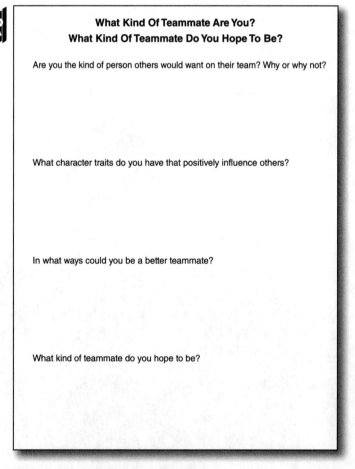

Figure 2.3   Reflection worksheet.

- Are you the kind of person others would want on their team? Why or why not?
- What character traits do you have that positively impact others?
- In what ways could you be a better teammate?
- What kind of teammate do you hope to be?

This is a personal process that shouldn't be shared with others. This activity could serve as good baseline data to be recorded in personal journals or portfolios. To measure growth, the same document should be completed at the end of the team-building unit or end of the year.

Facilitating a Growth Mindset

Participants will inevitably experience failure when attempting team-building challenges. If they are taught to approach obstacles as opportunities and failure as an important factor in success, they will have the mindset needed to positively navigate through conflict. Individuals who maintain a growth mindset understand that hard work and adversity are essential to growth and learning. In contrast, people with a fixed mindset believe that talents and abilities are static; if you can't do it now, you will never be able to do it. As a result, they often give up easily and avoid taking risks. If we want our students and teams to reach their full potential, we must help them develop a growth mindset.

Start by introducing the language of a growth and fixed mindset. See table 2.1 for examples.

There are a number of websites and YouTube videos that creatively explain what a growth mindset looks like and sounds like, including the following:

- ClassDojo growth mindset
- Michael Jordan "Failure" Nike Commercial
- On the Road with Steve Hartman, CBS (these are two stories of many that demonstrate a growth mindset):
  - "Diving in the world of the unknown, student-athlete proves the merits of hard work."
  - "Teen who lost his hands makes three-pointers on basketball court"
- ABC: America Strong has several inspirational stories of perseverance

A Y-chart discussion about growth mindset will also help students grasp these concepts. Ask students daily to reflect on how a growth mindset was demonstrated in class. Continually reflect and reinforce the desired behaviors you'd like to see in your students. When you see or hear examples of a growth mindset in class, point it out and celebrate!

Once students understand a growth versus fixed mindset, allow them to reflect on their own mindset (see figure 2.4).

Keep these self-reflections and hand them back periodically throughout the unit or year. Allow students to revisit the three things they plan to do to maintain

Table 2.1   Language of Fixed Mindset and Growth Mindset

Fixed Mindset	Growth Mindset
This is too hard.	This may take some time and effort, but I bet I can figure it out.
I give up.	I'll use some of the strategies I've learned, and I will keep trying.
It's good enough.	Is this really my best work?
I'm not good at this.	I'm on the right track; if I keep working, I know I will get better.
I made a mistake.	Mistakes help me improve.
I don't understand.	What am I missing, and how can I figure it out?
I lost again.	Even though I lost the game, I learned what I can do better next time.

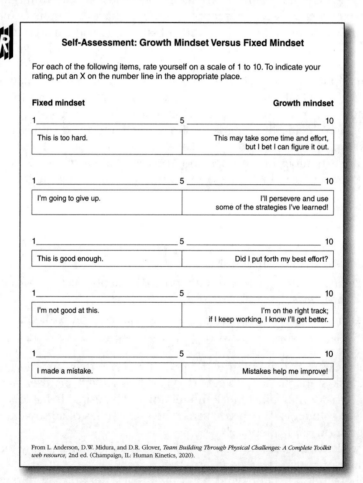

Figure 2.4   Self-assessment for growth mindset versus fixed mindset.

a growth mindset. Are they following through? Would they rate themselves higher than they did at the beginning of the year? Allow students to complete an evaluation at the end of the unit or year to measure growth.

Once students have a good understanding of what a growth mindset is, help them make the connection between having a growth mindset and team building through physical challenges. Consider asking the following questions:

- In team building, you will experience failure when attempting the challenges. Why are we learning about a growth mindset before beginning team building?
- Why is it important to maintain a growth mindset?
- If your team fails while attempting a challenge, how would someone with a growth mindset handle it?
- How might someone with a fixed mindset handle a failed attempt?
- How would your team handle it if a team member had a fixed mindset?

Students need to understand that failure is often our best teacher IF we have a growth mindset. If we have a fixed mindset, then failure and obstacles become excuses to quit.

Teaching Effective Praise and Encouragement

An excellent way to teach students how to be supportive, optimistic teammates is to teach them how to effectively praise and encourage. When students learn to recognize positive actions or character traits in others, they are learning how to think more optimistically. What a gift to be able to identify the strengths in others and then tell them! In addition, participants will be more likely to take risks when they understand their teammates are not going to blame them or get mad when mistakes are made. Trust is strengthened when teammates build each other up, especially in challenging situations. Not only are students learning how to be supportive teammates through learning how to praise and encourage but also praise is a great way to motivate and reinforce desired behaviors and skills.

Feedback is too often negative, whether it be from a teacher, coach, or teammate. Negative feedback can hurt the recipient, which in turn can have a negative impact on the team. There is a difference between honest, constructive feedback—which is very important—and negative feedback. Constructive feedback and praise play a big part in motivation and growth. Unfortunately, leaders underestimate the power of praise. It can be extremely motivating when it's specific, genuine, and effort based. False or generic praise can produce negative results, such as always needing or seeking approval.

Author and psychologist Carol Dweck researched the correlation between praise and motivation. Through her research, she learned that praising intelligence or abilities alone encourages a fixed mindset. In contrast, praising effort, perseverance, engagement—factors that an individual can control—fosters a growth mindset and increases motivation. Praising the positive behaviors that lead to the outcome is more motivational than praising only the final outcome. Use sentences such as these to praise behaviors rather than outcomes:

- "We won this game because we *didn't give up. We worked through frustration and learned from the mistakes* we made."
- "It was a long hard battle, but you continued to *work hard and do your best.*"
- "You were successful because you *worked together.* You *made good passes,* you *encouraged each other,* and everyone *put the team first.*"

Modeling effective praise is the best way to teach it. However, as with any skill, praise needs to be taught, practiced, and reinforced. Praising others is not a natural thing to do, even for adults. Consider the following process:

Leader: "Praising others is a powerful skill to have, but it's also hard to do. It doesn't come naturally, especially if we don't practice. Not many kids or adults take the time to praise others. At the same time, we all enjoy being praised. Praise involves recognizing positive actions or behaviors in others and then telling them. All too often, we miss out on building up our teammates because we don't know how to praise, because we choose not to praise, or because we are too uncomfortable to praise; instead, we avoid praise altogether. Think of how you feel when someone praises you. Now think about how often you praise others. If it's not too often, that's okay! You are going to learn how to praise, and then we are going to practice so it becomes more natural and comfortable."

Ask students for examples of praise phrases. Responses might include "good job," "way to go," "you are awesome," and "nice going."

Leader: "Those are great phrases, and we may feel good when we hear them, but you are going to learn how to praise specific positive behaviors that contribute to teamwork and effort. For example, instead of just saying, 'Good job,' you might say, 'Good job, Sanai. I saw you encouraging your team after a tough first half.' You could also say, 'Nice going, Hana. You got those offensive rebounds because you outworked your opponent.' Notice that I praised both the qualities that make a good teammate (encouragement) and effort (outworked your opponent)."

Share the positive adjectives sheet with students (see figure 2.5) or allow the class to create a list; use this sheet or list when students have difficulty coming up with their own words. Read through all the words and make sure students understand the meanings.

Positive adjectives should be shared using the following formula:

[Name], *you are* [adjective] *because* [specific reason related to effort or teamwork].

For example,

"Vincent, *you are* creative *because* when we need to come up with a new plan or strategy, you always have great ideas."

Positive Adjectives

Kind	Neat	Strong
Nice	Happy	Active
Cheerful	Courteous	Honest
Clever	Inventive	Imaginative
Enthusiastic	Helpful	Patient
Bright	Thoughtful	Determined
Convincing	Wise	Creative
Independent	Humorous	Pleasant
Delightful	Calm	Confident
Friendly	Inclusive	Empathic
Tolerant	Funny	Caring
Compassionate	Generous	Outgoing

You are _____ because _____.

From L. Anderson, D.W. Midura, and D.R. Glover, *Team Building Through Physical Challenges: A Complete Toolkit web resource*, 2nd ed. (Champaign, IL: Human Kinetics, 2020).

Figure 2.5 Positive adjectives sheet.

Give the class the opportunity to practice. Bring a student up to the front of the room. Give the group a minute to think about what the student does well, either as a teammate or in work ethic. Tell the group, "I'd like each person to pick an adjective on the sheet that describes [student's name]. Be prepared to share the reason you chose that adjective and how it relates to effort or teamwork. Say the student's name then say, 'You are.' Then share the adjective you chose and why you chose it. You don't just say, 'Vincent, you are creative.' You say, 'Vincent, you are creative *because…*' Always share specific behaviors or actions that describe the adjective you chose."

This is not an easy concept, and it must be practiced in a safe setting for it to become more natural. A good way to practice is to choose one student a week; at the end of each week, all students will share their praise statement for the selected student or have four to five students share their praise statements each day throughout the week for the selected student. When everyone has had the opportunity to share, choose another student.

This is an important concept for many reasons. Students positively praise others, but the person being praised often has no idea their classmates or teammates feel the way they do. Hearing people share the positive character traits they notice does wonders for confidence. It's also a great relationship-building activity. Finally, by sharing the specific reasons that describe the chosen positive adjective, desired behaviors or actions are continually being reinforced. This is one of the best behavior-management techniques there is—proactively facilitating an understanding of positive behaviors in a student-led approach.

There are many different ways to practice praise. Have students put their name on a piece of paper and place the papers in a hat. Each student would then pick a name out of the hat. Students should not tell anyone whose name they picked. Throughout the week, they look for ways their person demonstrated good effort or teamwork. Each day, two or three students publicly praise their person. Remember, the word *because* needs to be included in the praise statements.

These techniques need to be modeled by the leader as much as possible. In addition, reflect on the positive praise heard throughout the class period. The more praising others is modeled, practiced, and reinforced, the more it will become a natural behavior.

Encouragement and Growth Mindset

Teaching the importance of encouragement, and how to encourage, contributes to a stronger emotional intelligence and facilitates a growth mindset. Asking participants to reflect about how well they manage their emotions in happy, stressful, and frustrating times is a good place to start. Teaching students how to encourage will help build resilient teams who unite in challenging situations instead of breakdown when times get tough. By learning how to encourage and manage frustrating emotions, students are learning positive ways to react to negative feelings. Ask students the following reflective questions to help them better understand how they feel and react when frustration sets in:

- What are some situations that make you frustrated?
- How do you feel when frustration sets in?
- How do you typically handle frustration?
- What are some things that help you work through your frustration?
- Are there things people say or do that make you feel worse?
- Are there things people say or do that make you feel better?

Tell students, "When we try something new or challenging, it's likely mistakes will be made and obstacles will be met. We have to recognize that this is a good thing! If we never try things that are tough for us, we won't get better. It's through failure and challenges that we grow the most. It's okay to get frustrated in these situations; it's a natural feeling! How you react to that frustration determines the final outcome. Do you try and maintain a growth mindset, realizing that it's hard work and effort that help you succeed? Or do you get down on yourself or others; do you say or do something inappropriate or possibly even quit?"

When students begin to recognize how they feel and react to their own frustration, they will better understand how others feel in difficult or frustrating times. This process develops empathy, which is where encouragement comes in. Tell students, "Think of how you feel when you are frustrated. Think of what others do or say to help you get through it. Just imagine if you were the kind of teammate who helped your team overcome adversity through your words or actions instead of making it worse by impulsively reacting. It's not easy when a teammate makes a mistake that causes the team to lose or fall behind. Before we take the time to think of how badly that person must feel, we often react to our own frustration and say or do something that makes the situation worse. This often leads to team breakdown. Instead, what could you do to build up your teammates after mistakes are made or setbacks occur?"

Ask students to brainstorm ideas and complete a Y-chart. Ask the group this question: What does encouragement look like, sound like, and feel like? This could be done as a whole group or in small groups whose ideas are eventually shared with the whole group.

Tell students, "Encouragement is all about building others up when they are down or facing a challenge. It's encouraging a growth mindset. Encouragement makes others more determined, hopeful, or confident; with determination, hope, and confidence, they are more likely to do challenging things they are afraid they can't do. Think of the people in your life who have this special ability of building others up. What do they do or say? Think of the powerful impact you could have on the team by helping others feel more determined or confident. Wow! Instead of reacting to your own emotions and tearing down a teammate or making him or her feel worse, recognize that he or she may need support and encouragement and then provide it."

Take some time to brainstorm encouraging phrases. Possibilities might include the following phrases:

- "Keep going!"
- "Give it another try!"
- "Don't give up!"
- "You can do it!"
- "Let's work together!"

Ask students for nonverbal examples of encouragement. Possibilities might include the following nonverbal expressions:

- Thumbs-up
- Fist bump
- Pat on the back
- High five
- Smile

Post these examples of the students' ideas on the gym or classroom wall.

Older students can practice praise and encouragement while practicing basketball skills. Specifically, while one student practices shooting, the rebounders and passers can practice praise and encouragement. Set up five poly spots in an arc around the basket; the distance from the basket should be determined by the age of the students. Organize the students in the following manner.

- One student is designated as the shooter. The shooter's job is to make a shot from each poly spot within a three-minute span.

- Two students are designated as rebounders. Their job is to retrieve the ball after each shot and get it to one of the two passers.
- Appoint two other students as the passers. Once a passer receives the ball, he or she passes it to the shooter for another attempt. This process continues until either the shooter makes a shot from each poly spot or the three-minute time limit is met.

During the activity, the rebounders and passers provide specific praise and encouragement to the shooter. Appoint another student (or two) per group to fulfill the role of recorder. The recorder's job is to note all specific praise and encouragement, verbal and nonverbal phrases, on the social skills observation sheet (see figure 2.6).

Rotate as many times as possible (you may want to give everyone a chance to shoot). Decide how to rotate shooters, but remember that the recorders do not rotate. After a set amount of rotations, bring the class together and have the recorders report all praise and encouragement that was noted.

Social Skills Observation

Name	See	Hear

From L. Anderson, D.W. Midura, and D.R. Glover, *Team Building Through Physical Challenges: A Complete Toolkit web resource*, 2nd ed. (Champaign, IL: Human Kinetics, 2020).

Figure 2.6   Social skills observation sheet.

Doing, Practicing, and Reflecting

Reflection is an excellent teaching tool but often a forgotten component of learning. We learn by doing, but we learn even more by doing *and* reflecting. Our experiences, successes, trials, and errors are often our best teachers if we take the time to reflect and learn from them. Students are too often told what they are doing right or wrong and what they need to do to improve. In this case, the teacher, coach, or leader is doing all the thinking. The best learning comes when students do the reflecting; that's where valuable learning takes place. Critical-thinking skills are facilitated when students analyze their behaviors and actions and problem solve solutions or improvements.

Ask a reflective question at the end of every class period. If encouragement is being taught and practiced, then ask, "What were some encouraging phrases that were used in class today?" Through reflection and reinforcement, the desired skills are better understood and retained by students if they can make connections on a daily basis.

General reflective questions that can be asked in a variety of situations are listed below:

- In what ways did your words or actions impact your team today?
- How did you use praise and encouragement today?
- How did you feel after a teammate praised or encouraged you?
- Our word of the week is integrity. Who can share some examples of integrity that were demonstrated today?
- How did your team handle failed attempts?
- What are you most proud of today?
- What are some things you hope to do differently next time?
- What did you learn from your mistakes today?
- What did you learn from your successes today?

Authentic learning experiences are created when students connect the desired skills to their own behaviors and actions. When they reflect on what went well and what they might do differently next time, they are working toward continual improvement.

Participants now understand what good teamwork looks like, sounds like, and feels like. They understand how to recognize the strengths in their teammates, they know how to build each other up in the face of adversity, and they know how to maintain a growth mindset. They have been set up for success; now let's give them the opportunity to practice by placing them in teams.

Forming Teams

Our experience has shown that teams of six to eight have the optimum number of participants for team-building challenges. Groups of fewer than six tend to experience less struggle in achieving success, whereas groups larger than eight simply have too much waiting time during the group activities.

How groups are created is up to the leader's discretion. To save time, groups can be created in advance, or participants can be placed randomly when they get to class. As leaders, you know your group the best. Think proactively about how to create teams that can succeed.

Constructing a Team Pact

The first activity for teams is to plan how they are going to be successful. They should do this activity before starting the challenges. Tell students, "Your team needs to come up with guidelines to ensure success. What needs to happen with each teammate for your team to function as positively and productively as possible? Think about what we have discussed. What did you learn about the characteristics of a good team member? With these questions in mind, you can come up with some guidelines for your team's success. These guidelines are going to be called your Team Pact. Once you have finalized your Team Pact and everyone agrees on it, each team member needs to sign it. Determine a fair way to designate who will be the recorder for your team." Each team should come up with at least five guidelines. The following is an example of a student-created Team Pact:

- We will listen to each other.
- We will let every team member have a chance to talk or share ideas.
- We will encourage each other if things get hard or we make mistakes.
- We will all work hard and stay on task.
- There will be no put-downs.

By signing our names, we commit to following our Team Pact and supporting our teammates to the best of our ability.

Selecting Team Names

To strengthen the sense of connection and unity, each team should determine a team name. Conflicts can occur if teammates don't agree on ideas, so ask proactive questions to help participants positively handle disagreements ("How is your team going to handle it if you disagree on the team name?"). By anticipating challenges and allowing participants to determine solutions, teams are being set up for success. Consider the following guidelines for determining a team name:

- The name should reflect work ethic, thinking abilities, teamwork, or a positive attitude.
- The name should be positive or neutral in nature (no negative names).
- The name can be humorous.
- The name can relate to terms studied in academic units or may possibly have a geographic relationship to the group.

We encourage our teams to come up with names that reflect thinking abilities, a positive attitude, effort, teamwork, or good character. For example, encourage names such as The Persevering Seven, The Prideful Eight, Dynamic Dendrites, The Leaping Leaders, or The Positive Peeps. However, you decide what's appropriate for your program and whether or not general names such as the Bears are acceptable. Examples of names we have vetoed are Mega Brain Death, The No Minds, The Dweebs, Dumb and Dumber, and The Brain Tumors.

Team-Building Roles

Opportunities to practice leadership during team building are plentiful. The participant roles that we feel are important to the team-building process are the organizer, encourager, praiser, summarizer, and recorder. These roles should rotate among teammates after each challenge or each new day challenges are attempted. The purpose of assigning these roles is to set up participants for success and allow each team member to experience and practice being a leader. Too often it's the best athletes or the most outgoing students who are perceived as leaders by their peers. When students are assigned leadership roles, they are provided the opportunity to shine.

Organizer

When the team approaches a challenge, they will see two cards—a challenge card and an organizer card. Examples are shown in figure 2.7; all challenge cards and organizer cards for most of the challenges in this book are available on the web resource. You may want to print and laminate these cards and place them by the appropriate challenge. The organizer card includes a series of questions designed to help group members understand what was read on the challenge card, which describes the basic requirements of the challenge.

The organizer reads the challenge card to the team or passes it to someone else if he or she feels uncomfortable reading. This act of decision making puts the organizer in a leadership position. If the organizer decides to read the card to the team, the leadership role expands. Talking to the team and explaining a challenge through these cards is a leadership experience that team building provides. It's important to set the organizer up for success and brainstorm potential problems that may occur while the organizer is reading the card. For example, students may not listen, or the organizer might speak too quietly. Ask simple questions such as these: "Teams, what is your responsibility while the organizer is reading the card? Where should your eyes be? What should you do if you cannot hear the organizer?" This also may be a good opportunity for a Y-Chart if your class has a hard time understanding the organizer's role.

If teams are unable to answer the questions to clarify they understand the challenge, the organizer should patiently review the parts of the challenge card that need clarification. Once this step is complete, the group may then attempt to solve the challenge. One reason for using this element in preparation is to help the group focus clearly on the rules and sacrifices. It is quite discouraging for a group to begin solving the challenge and then be held accountable for informa-

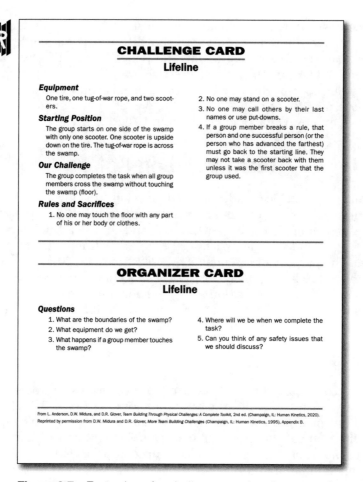

Figure 2.7 Examples of a challenge card and an organizer card for the Lifeline challenge.

tion that wasn't understood. The instructor should not be solely responsible for enforcing the rules of a challenge. A group should have the integrity to acknowledge and follow through on the listed consequence after a rule has been broken.

Encourager

By definition, to encourage is to give others courage. The role of encourager is a very important role and likely the most difficult. It's when times are most challenging that the encourager needs to step up. Team members may start hanging their heads or get down on each other after failed attempts; the encourager needs to use the strategies he or she learned to build up the team. Emotional intelligence comes into play in these situations. We hope that all group members will eventually take this role without it being assigned. An encourager's job is to find encouraging words to inspire teammates while the group is attempting the challenge or working through frustration. The role of encourager is ongoing throughout the task.

Praiser

The praiser should find at least one specific act related to effort or teamwork to praise before the completion of the challenge. For example, if a teammate makes a good suggestion or helps another student, the praiser should acknowledge that act by saying, "Bobby, good idea; it really helped our team solve the challenge." A praiser should be sincere. Generic or false praise can have a negative impact. Ideally, everyone will start praising before long, allowing the elimination of the roles of praiser and encourager. The role of praiser is ongoing throughout the task.

The roles of praiser and encourager offer another opportunity for leadership. Remember, however, the act of praising and encouraging do not come naturally. It's very important to continually practice. In the beginning, assign the roles to students who may be more comfortable. Some teachers assign roles by asking for volunteers.

Summarizer (Optional)

The role of summarizer can either be for an individual or the whole team. The summarizer provides an account of how the team solved the challenge, how teamwork was demonstrated, what challenges the team overcame, and what the key elements were to achieving success. The summarizer can be given a team report card (see example in chapter 3). You can modify the team report card to meet the needs of your group or to achieve a desired scope of discussion.

Recorder (Optional)

The recorder highlights specific praise and encouragement that the group used during the challenge, which reinforces those desired skills we are trying to facilitate in our students. The recorder can give the recording sheets to the teacher after reporting, and the teacher can put them on the bulletin board. Once the teacher feels the class is proficient in the skills of praising and encouraging, recording phrases may no longer be necessary, or perhaps it's done periodically throughout the year.

Leader's Role in Team Building

The leader needs to avoid solving the challenges and serve as a facilitator when necessary. Although it can be tempting to offer help to teams, especially those experiencing frustration, discouragement, or failure, teams should be encouraged to collaboratively problem solve through the obstacles. By proactively teaching students and teams how to maintain a growth mindset prior to attempting the challenges, participants will be much more successful when facing adversity. There will, however, still be conflict. The leader should ask questions to help students better problem solve solutions. Allow team members to fail. If they understand that failure provides the best learning opportunities, they will be less likely to blame others or quit. Be a good observer and model praise and encouragement. When you see good examples of teamwork and resilience, model positive praise by pointing them out and enthusiastically celebrating!

We recommend that leaders give as little help as possible during these activities. The struggle involved in the process of success is of great value. Helping the group solve the challenge defeats the purpose of team building and collaboratively working through challenges. Don't allow discipline issues with students to become excuses to quit team building. Model a growth mindset by expecting conflict and using the strategies mentioned in this chapter to minimize or resolve it.

Setting Up Activity Spaces and Equipment

Be sure to set out the correct equipment for the teams prior to each challenge. Look over all safety concerns and arrangements. Examine the figures in the book and read the challenge descriptions to ensure that you place the equipment in the correct or suitable places.

We recommend setting up more stations than you have participating groups. When working in a school setting in which we have three or four groups in a class, we set up one more station than we have groups. That way, groups who finish a challenge can proceed to the next one.

The challenges in this book are designed to use equipment that is either readily available or economical to purchase. As you look through the challenges presented in this book, we feel confident that you will be able to obtain most of the items without difficulty.

The gymnasium is typically the most optimal space for conducting team-building activities. However, we have also used spaces such as lunchrooms, classrooms, outdoor playground areas, meeting rooms in motel or hotel facilities, sanctuaries of churches, ballrooms and hallways in casinos, stage areas, beaches, and other spaces where we simply moved out tables, chairs, and other equipment to create a large, open space.

With a little creativity, you can modify any challenge to meet your needs. For example, in the Black Hole challenge in chapter 8, you can easily suspend a hula hoop from a basketball hoop. If you are in a space that does not have a basketball hoop, you may have to suspend the hoop from a ceiling structure or an overhead beam or railing. If you do this task outdoors, suspend it from a structure such as a football goal post or playground equipment such as a swing set.

Most challenges that we are presenting simply need adequate room for travel or movement. The ceiling need not be as high as a gymnasium. A large, open room such as a recreation hall, lunchroom, or dance floor offers the same functionality as a basketball court. The size of your group will determine how many challenges you set up at one time. Additionally, some challenges require very little room to conduct. We have observed classroom teachers move all desks to the perimeter of a classroom and set up Stepping Stones I (see chapter 7), Stepping Stones II (see chapter 8), The Maze (see chapter 7), Construction Zone (see chapter 6), and Building Blocks (see chapter 7). Hallways of buildings can accommodate challenges such as Tire Bridge and Lifeline (see chapter 6), which require long, narrow work areas.

Selecting Appropriate Activities and Challenges

People often ask us why all groups should not do the same challenges at the same time. The main reason is simply that you are not likely to have enough of the same equipment to set up three or more similar stations at one time. A more practical approach is to set up a few challenges of equal difficulty. As an example, in the first few meetings of your teams, they may all attempt introductory challenges. We have not set up the individual challenges in a sequential order. Instead, we have grouped the challenges into three levels of difficulty: introductory, intermediate, and advanced. The beginning challenges do not require nearly as much physical support among teammates or as much planning and problem solving as the intermediate and advanced challenges. Choose a number of challenges by level as you prepare your groups for their tasks. In addition, the equipment that you have at your disposal will dictate the challenges that you present to your participants.

Summary

Team building through physical challenges is an excellent way to learn teamwork and a growth mindset. However, before attempting the challenges, it's essential to facilitate the skills necessary to be optimistic, supportive teammates and resilient, unified teams. Students and athletes will have long-lasting memories from team building through physical challenges because of the emotions elicited. They will remember the feelings of significance and acceptance that comes from belonging to a team, the pride and confidence that results from persevering through adversity, and the joy and enthusiasm associated with taking risks and eventually succeeding. More importantly, the skills your students or athletes take away from team building through physical challenges will benefit them for a lifetime—both personally and professionally.

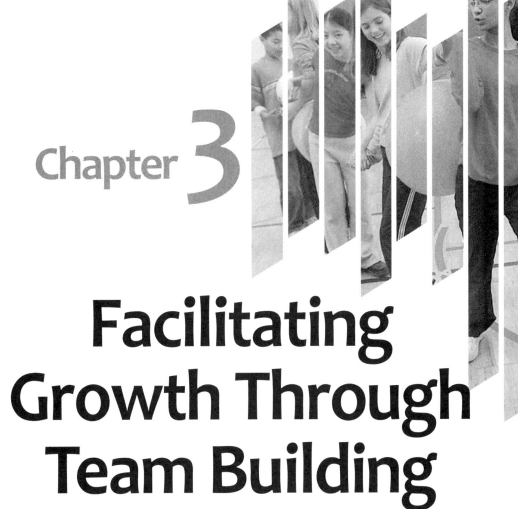

Chapter 3

Facilitating Growth Through Team Building and Assessment

Learning is strengthened when students are actively involved in the learning process. When given a voice, students feel empowered, and motivation increases. Self-assessment is one of the most valuable ways to involve learners. By evaluating their own work and making adjustments based on past mistakes and successes, students learn how to be critical thinkers and problem solvers. In the process, they also gain a deeper understanding of the content being taught.

This chapter focuses on the importance of using assessment as a tool to enrich and strengthen learning, not just as a means to determine a grade or score.

All too often, assessment is used as mode of measurement by the instructor, who then provides feedback to the student. In this case, the instructor is the one who engages in critical thinking, and the student misses out on valuable learning opportunities. Assessment is a powerful strategy to enrich learning—if the student is an active participant. The following self-assessment questions encourage higher-level thinking, which in turn increases understanding:

- What am I most proud of?
- What could I improve?
- What was my biggest challenge, and how did I overcome it?
- Compared to the set criteria or rubrics, what score do I deserve and why?
- What improvements will I make?
- What was my biggest takeaway?

There is a definite place for instructor feedback, but teaching students how to be critical thinkers is one of the most valuable concepts that can be taught in any field of study. In his article titled "Teachers Say Critical Thinking Key to College and Career Readiness," Louis Freedberg (2015) indicates that "Teachers overwhelmingly supported the goal of preparing students for college and careers. When asked to rank the most important indicators of college and career readiness, 78 percent of teachers ranked developing critical thinking skills among the three most important indicators." Freedberg's article also highlights the shared belief of college professors that the ability to think critically is a more valuable indicator of success than a score on a test. "The disagreement would come from admissions officers who find tests very efficient in deciding who is eligible for admission or not."

With the pressure on teachers to provide a grade or score, teaching critical-thinking skills is often not an emphasis. How do you "grade" another person's ability to reflect or think critically? These skills are much more difficult to grade or score, so they are simply not a priority. Even with the wealth of knowledge supporting the importance of college and career readiness skills, memorization is still one of the most common practices in teaching and learning, likely because it's the easiest to grade. Ironically, memorization is also one of the least effective techniques in learning.

Reflection

Self-assessment requires reflective thinking, which is another essential, underused teaching and learning tool. Both concepts are key factors that contribute to the successful completion of the team-building challenges.

In the pursuit of succeeding in team-building challenges, teams learn how to communicate and brainstorm creative solutions. After failed attempts, teams learn how to take a step back, analyze the situation, reflect on what went well and what went wrong, and then form possible solutions. Teaching participants to be creative in their thinking allows them to be better problem solvers. Teaching creative-thinking skills, however, is another facet of learning often overlooked due to the complexities of grading in education. At the same time, creative thinking skills are some of the most sought-after skills in the 21st-century workplace.

In the process of completing the challenges, participants will naturally practice critical thinking, problem solving, teamwork, and communicating. They also will learn how to maintain a growth mindset and embrace mistakes and roadblocks. Team building through physical challenges is an excellent way to learn how to overcome failure and proactively plan for success. To do so, time needs to be taken to evaluate progress and determine what improvements or changes need to be made. This is often one of the most difficult concepts relating to the physical challenges. Children, and many adults, have a hard time slowing down and assessing progress.

In our years of experience with leading team-building physical challenges, we've learned that participants develop the following skills:

Teamwork

- Put forth your best effort at all times.
- Recognize your impact on the team.
- Encourage and support teammates in times of adversity.
- Value team goals over individual goals.
- Recognize each teammate's unique value and contribution.

Growth Mindset

- Recognize failure and adversity as valuable learning opportunities.
- Approach challenging situations with optimism and determination.
- Apply time and effort to solving problems and overcoming challenges.

Communication and Leadership

- Contribute suggestions and ideas with respect.
- Listen to and value the suggestions and ideas of others.
- Provide verbal and nonverbal support and encouragement.
- Fulfill the responsibilities of praiser, encourager, organizer, summarizer, and recorder.
- Demonstrate self-control and model a growth mindset.

Critical Thinking and Problem Solving

- Make decisions based on which ideas are working and which are not.
- Problem solve through conflicts in team dynamics.
- Collaboratively work through failure and adversity.
- Recognize and tap into the unique strengths of each individual when creating a plan to solve each challenge.

It's crucial for students to explore their own level of understanding if we want students to improve in these valuable skills as they participate in team-building challenges. Figure 3.1 is a team-building self-evaluation that facilitates an understanding of key concepts being taught. Through reflection, participants recognize their own growth and understanding in these concepts. This self-evaluation

Team-Building Self-Evaluation

Rate yourself in the areas below. You are not graded on this evaluation, but it's important your scores reflect your honest thoughts.

Scores range from 1-5. One being you are performing at a low level or have little understanding and five means you are performing at a high level. Place an X on line indicating your score.

Teamwork

I put team goals ahead of personal goals.

1_____2_____3_____4_____5

I work hard at all times because I know my efforts directly impact my team.

1_____2_____3_____4_____5

I praise my teammates when positive things happen and encourage my teammates when facing challenging situations.

1_____2_____3_____4_____5

I value all of my teammates and recognize that they each play an important role on the team.

1_____2_____3_____4_____5

In the area of teamwork, I am most proud
of_____
_____.

In the area of teamwork, I need to work
on_____
_____.

From L. Anderson, D.W. Midura, and D.R. Glover, *Team Building Through Physical Challenges: A Complete Toolkit web resource,* 2nd ed. (Champaign, IL: Human Kinetics, 2020).

Figure 3.1   Team-building self-evaluation.

can be used as both a pre-assessment and post-assessment for the team-building unit; allowing students to rate themselves at the beginning of the unit provides a good baseline, and allowing them to complete it again at the end of the unit helps them recognize and reflect on how much they have grown.

It's also important to have teams collaboratively reflect on how well they work together.

Verbally completing a team report card (see figure 3.2) at the end of each challenge provides the continual opportunity to focus on the desired skills and make necessary adjustments.

For teams to be successful, individuals need to sacrifice personal agendas for the best interest of the team. Teams must collaboratively set goals and recognize that teamwork has a huge impact on whether goals will be met. Teams grow stronger and continuously improve when they routinely reflect on progress made toward goals and learn how to build on what's going well and tweak what's not.

Figure 3.2 Team report card.

Weekly Reflection

Weekly reflections are called a number of names, such as learning logs, growth logs, goal trackers, and reflective journals. By any name, the point of such activities is to track growth and provide opportunities to reflect and make improvements. Prompting students to engage in reflective activities is a great way to track growth, strengthen learning, and reinforce a growth mindset.

Before expecting students to become reflective learners, however, we must teach them how to do so. At first, students often struggle with reflection because they have rarely been given the opportunity. Instead, they are typically told what they are doing right or wrong and how to improve. Rather, if we help develop a daily or weekly habit of reflection, participants quickly gain the skills and appreciate the opportunity. Figure 3.3 shows a sample weekly reflection you can use to show students how to walk through the process of reflecting on their work.

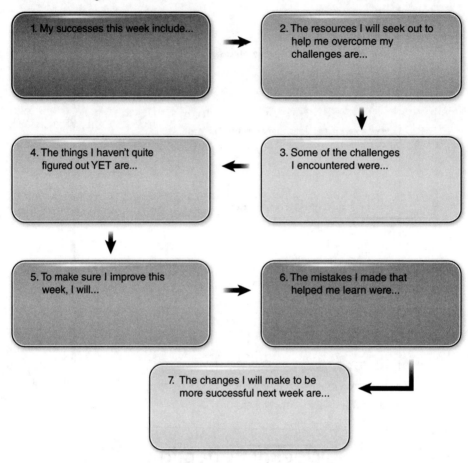

Figure 3.3   Sample weekly reflection.

Goal Setting

Effective goal setting can help students and teams maximize performance. Following through on goals by regularly assessing and tracking progress makes goal setting a meaningful process. All too often, goals are set and then ignored. When teachers and coaches ask students and teams to set goals, they do so with the best intentions. Inadvertently, however, the "full speed ahead" mentality kicks in, and we often fail to prioritize the power of slowing down and going deeper.

Success breeds motivation. When students and teams are given the opportunity to track their growth and celebrate their successes along the way, they are intrinsically motivated to continue striving for improvement. At the same time, reaching a goal typically comes at an expense. Sacrifices are made, setbacks occur, and frustration often sets in. If students learn to anticipate and embrace these challenges, they will be more likely to persevere through them and less likely to use them as excuses to quit.

The most popular format for goal setting is the SMART format. SMART goals are S-specific, M-measurable, A-attainable or achievable, R-realistic, and T-time bound. There is no question that using this model is an effective way to set goals. However, it's important to emphasize achieving the goal, which requires monitoring and accountability, just as much as setting it. Figure 3.4 provides a proactive goal-setting guide that addresses the obstacles that are inevitably encountered while pursuing a goal, along with the resources needed to find solutions.

Tracking progress is a part of goal setting that often gets overlooked. Making continual progress requires being intentional about tracking growth. Take the time to slow down, assess, and document successes and challenges. While setting the goal, participants will determine how often, and when, they will assess progress and what tracking tool will be used. Figure 3.5 provides an example of how to track progress toward goals, whether it be on a daily, weekly, or monthly basis.

GROWTH Goal-Setting Guide

G:	Goal	What is the specific goal I/we want to accomplish by what date?
		What is the starting point? Include baseline data and information.
R:	Realistic Plan	How?
		When?
		Where?
		Who?
O:	Obstacles	Proactively thinking, what potential obstacles might we encounter?
		How will I/we recognize these obstacles as learning opportunities and not as excuses to quit?

From L. Anderson, D.W. Midura, and D.R. Glover, *Team Building Through Physical Challenges: A Complete Toolkit web resource*, 2nd ed. (Champaign, IL: Human Kinetics, 2020).

Figure 3.4   GROWTH goal-setting guide.

GROWTH Tracking				
Date:	Attempting (beginning)	Almost there (continued effort needed)	Yes! I'm where I need to be to reach my goal.	I'm doing better than I thought! I've exceeded my own expectations.
G: Goal How is my overall progress toward reaching my goal?				
R: Realistic Plan Do my choices support the plan I have in place?				
O: Obstacles Am I learning as a result of the obstacles I encounter?				
W: Who and What? Have I been resourceful when setbacks have occurred? Have I prevented obstacles from becoming excuses?				
T: Tracking Am I tracking my growth in a journal to measure it?				
H: Habits What new habits am I forming that contribute to my success?				
What is going well that I need to continue? What changes need to be made in order to reach my goal?				

From L. Anderson, D.W. Midura, and D.R. Glover, *Team Building Through Physical Challenges: A Complete Toolkit web resource*, 2nd ed. (Champaign, IL: Human Kinetics, 2020).

Figure 3.5   GROWTH tracking.

Portfolios

Student portfolios are a helpful tool for measuring and tracking growth. A portfolio is a collection of work or performance data that illustrates effort, growth, and achievement. The collection could include assessments and evaluations, sharing of personal interests or observations, self or peer reflections, weekly learning logs, and work samples or critiques of projects. This assessment tool helps students move beyond memorization and move toward becoming critical thinkers by analyzing, reflecting, and evaluating. Portfolios allow students to become more actively engaged in their learning. Giving students a voice in their education is invaluable and empowering. Furthermore, we have observed that students are more likely to discuss their portfolio evaluations with their parents than discuss a particular grade. With traditional grades, students rarely have input and may lack understanding as to why it was given and what they can do to improve. "With portfolios, traditional teaching roles may not work. Teachers need to facilitate, guide, and offer choices rather than inform, direct and pre-determine priorities. Partnerships are established among teacher, students and parents" (Melograno 1998).

A successful portfolio demonstrates growth. Many use it simply as a scrap-book, collecting various pieces of work during the unit of study. Communicate growth by including baseline information before each unit of study. A baseline will show the skill or knowledge level at the start of a unit of study. To demon-strate growth, the data will then be compared to the end-of-the-unit evaluations, reflections, and assessments. It's tough to measure how far you have come if you don't have documentation to show where you started.

Summary

Authentic and meaningful learning experiences are created when students are involved in their learning. They are more motivated, engaged, and likely to put forth their best effort. Developing optimistic, supportive teammates and resilient, unified teams takes time and effort. For growth to be maximized, time needs to be set aside for individuals and teams to reflect, assess their skills, and track their growth. Assessment must be used as a tool for growth, not just as a tool to measure growth.

References

Freedberg, L. 2015. "Teachers Say Critical Thinking Key to College and Career Readiness." https://edsource.org/2015/teachers-say-critical-thinking-most-important-indicator-of-student-success/87810.

Melograno, V. 1998. *Professional and Student Portfolios for Physical Education* (Champaign, IL: Human Kinetics).

Chapter 4

Safety Strategies

Those of us who have spent years in the field of physical education or recreation always have safety on our minds when planning activities. The range of safety issues is virtually endless. The best advice we can offer is to think safety. No matter what activity we present, we can reinforce or teach methods of participation that reduce the risk factors of that particular activity. In this chapter, you will learn about general safety issues and guidelines relevant to team building and safety rules for specific tasks.

General Rules

In the challenges in this book, we include safety suggestions for each task. Rather than list each safety precaution, we present below some general safety rules or recommendations related specifically to team-building activities and challenges:

- Make sure that all participants understand the need for and importance of physical support during many of the challenges.
- The instructor should be aware of the physical limitations of all participants in the class. If some of the participants cannot physically accomplish a task, the instructor should make or offer adaptations.
- Pay close attention to activities that could potentially injure the head or neck. Point out the possibility of injury if participants attempt to solve the challenge

while disregarding safety practices. Point out the potential for injury for each challenge that contains elements of risk.

- Participants will be lifting objects such as tires, mats, other teammates, and so on. Discuss safety practices for lifting. Participants should lift by using the legs rather than the back.

- Before doing any challenges, the teams should always address safety concerns. The instructor can ask, "Have you thought of any potential safety issues that this challenge might present?" Other questions could focus on equipment— "How can we safely transfer a scooter? Could we get our fingers pinched using a scooter? How can we avoid a sore back from lifting tires?"

Besides these general rules, we list some safety concerns for each challenge as part of the description and administration of activities and challenges found in chapters 5 through 8.

Spotters and Spotting

Two types of spotting are needed to ensure safety and success in team building. The first type is the general concern that one teammate has for another. This awareness may consist of offering a hand to help a teammate maintain balance or giving someone a boost or helping hand to complete a challenge. This type of support shows care and concern for others. This type of help and support should become second nature to everyone involved in team building.

The second type of spotting requires participants to protect teammates from injury. This type of spotting means that teammates must trust one another. Without trust, members may not try challenges such as the Black Hole (see chapter 8), which requires participants to lift and pass teammates through a hoop. To build that trust among participants, convey the importance of spotting and impress upon teammates that fooling around during a difficult challenge diminishes trust among one another. Teach students how to lift and how to protect a teammate's head and neck so that everyone is safe.

Teaching Spotting

Spotting is an art. Know how and what to do in different situations to make the participants as safe as possible and have fun at the same time. Take an entire class period to practice these skills before the group attempts challenges in which people may be catching or lifting each other. This one class often brings the group together. As the instructor, you set the tone. If you make safety and proper spotting a priority, the participants will quickly follow your example. In those cases in which you do not have enough spotters for a challenge or for a particular person, postpone doing that event until you have adequate help. This is another way to emphasize the importance of participants' safety.

Tom Heck, the "Teach Me Teamwork" coach, developed the following pointers for teaching spotting:

- Explain the concept and meaning of spotting.
- Practice spotting with participants before they need to use the skill in an activity.

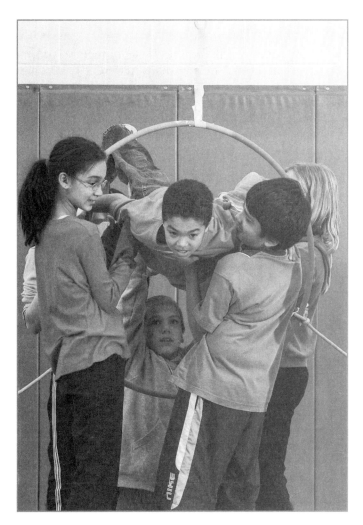

Establishing trust in team-building activities and challenges requires emotional and physical support from all team members.

- Promote the attitude that teasing and joking about not catching someone has no place in your program.
- Supervise spotters closely.
- Model proper spotting.
- A good spotter shares the responsibility of spotting equally. Working as a team when spotting is easier and safer.
- Spotters should stand in a balanced position, holding hands up in a ready position—or as some say, "Bumpers up." Spotters should focus on the participant.
- Spotters should cushion a fall, not catch and hold, and should move with the direction of force.

Courtesy of Tom Heck the "Teach Me Teamwork" coach on www.teachmeteamwork.com.

Spotting Guidelines

Spotting during team building will require the team members to recognize that teammates may need assistance during many different challenging situations. Teammates have to recognize when to spot and be ready to step in and help the teammates who need assistance. Spotting is a two-way communication process. The student needing a spot or assistance needs to "talk" to his or her teammates and tell them exactly what assistance is needed.

No matter what challenge a team is working to solve, there are four rules that should always be followed:

- Always protect the head and neck of the person you are spotting.
- While spotting, stand in a stride position.
- Participants and spotters should remove jewelry and watches as well as belts with large buckles.
- Teammates should always communicate when attempting a difficult challenge. Spotters should ask what the teammate attempting a challenge needs, and the teammate attempting a challenge should not be shy about asking for assistance.

Hoop and Swing Spotting

When spotting such activities as the Black Hole (see chapter 8), in which people go through a hanging hoop, "spotters" must follow these rules:

- Spot the head and neck of the person going through.
- Stay close to the person going through. The hoop might bump the spotters, but it won't hurt if the spotters stay close.
- Have your hands ready to catch or give support if the person going through needs protection.
- Keep your knees bent and move with the person going through and near the hoop.

Spotting people on a swinging event such as Grand Canyon, in which people must swing across a "canyon" via a hanging rope in the middle of the river, "spotters" must follow these rules:

- Stay focused on the person attempting the challenge.
- Stay close to the moving object so the spotter can avoid receiving a hard hit from the object and be in a position to protect the person who is going across.
- Have your hands ready to catch or spot, bend your knees, and have your feet in a stride position.

Note: Many people do not have the upper body strength to swing across an area by only holding on to a rope, or, on the first try, they might hold the rope incorrectly and fall off. To protect the person trying to swing across the canyon, lay a 2-inch-thick tumbling mat across the canyon to soften the landing if spotters are unable to break the fall.

If participants swing on a rope or walk across a balance beam, spotters should follow these rules:

- Stay close to the rope or beam.
- Focus on the person crossing.
- Have your hands ready to catch the person.

Standing on Another Person's Back

The person kneeling on the ground should have his or her knees under the hips and the arms directly under the shoulders. The back should be concave (arched downward).

The person standing on another person's back should have assistance when getting on and off. The feet should be placed over the hips and shoulders of the kneeling person down on all fours. The standing person should never place a foot on the lower back. This is the weakest part of the person's body. The standing person never should jump off the back because that would cause the kneeler to fall over and the jumper to lose his or her balance and fall.

We have made every effort to anticipate a variety of solutions to every challenge and to address safety issues. There is always a chance that a group will come up with a different solution, so the leader should keep safety in mind at all times.

Learning how to spot reinforces the belief among teammates that they must help protect and support their teammates. The instructor must emphasize the skill of spotting and teach students to lift with their legs, not their backs, and always be on the lookout for potential danger.

Equipment Safety

The first realm of concern is the equipment itself. Most of the equipment used for team building is easily obtained. Be sure to inspect the equipment for any safety issues (i.e., frayed ropes, poor wheels on scooters, or tires with exposed steel belts). Periodically inspect the equipment and store it safely.

Tires

We use automobile tires in many of the challenges. You can obtain them free of charge at virtually any establishment that sells or services tires. Additionally, you can recycle your own tires into your inventory of equipment and thus avoid paying the recycling fee attached to each purchase of a new tire. Be aware of exposed steel belts. Do not use any tire with exposed metal material (steel belts) that can cause a cut. We recommend washing used tires with soap and water both inside and out and then wiping off the tire with a car-care cleaning product such as Armor All. This process leaves the tires clean and usable so that they will not leave dirty marks on the floor, clothes, or hands. Smaller tires less than 13 inches (33 centimeters) in diameter are harder to find. We recommend looking for boat trailer or utility trailer tires at marine centers or auto centers that sell trailers. Some radial belt tires in these sizes still come without steel belts.

Ropes

In a number of our challenges, we use jump ropes in various ways. Our recommendation here is to use sash cord rope (the old-fashioned jump ropes). Many hardware stores, full-service home or lumber stores, and canvas warehouses carry this type of rope in 100-foot (30-meter) lengths (called hanks). These ropes are durable. Segmented ropes or the licorice-type jump ropes (also called speed ropes) may break if used for pulling teammates or equipment. If participants step on a rope, the rope could roll, causing them to twist an ankle.

Scooters

We use scooters in some challenges. We tend to use the standard 12-inch (30-centimeter) square scooter for most school-age students and the 16-inch (40-centimeter) square scooter for adults and students with special needs.

Each year, manufacturers seem to be making better wheels that allow users to travel farther with less effort, but this may not be desirable for our purpose. Before we discuss the travel issue, we caution you to forbid participants from standing on scooters at any time, even if they are certified skateboard professionals. Standing on scooters can lead to a variety of safety problems, so standing on

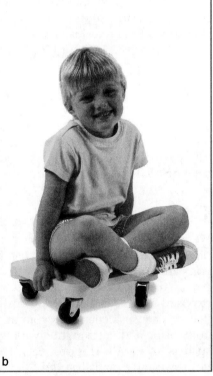

A *(a)* 16-inch and a *(b)* 12-inch scooter.
© Gopher Sport

them is forbidden. We have found that using older scooters that do not roll quite as easily as newer ones causes participants to work harder or find more ways to assist one another. This struggle is desirable in team-building challenges.

The misuse of scooters can include running over your own fingers or the fingers of others, being pushed off the scooter and landing unsafely on the floor (both forward and backward), and being pushed too fast or too far. We have never seen safety standards included with the purchase of scooters. Therefore, we recommend that you create a list of prudent safety items related to the careful use of scooters.

A few of our challenges that specify the use of scooters require, as part of the solution, the transfer of scooters from one student to another or from one group to another group. Students must demonstrate safe ways to transfer the scooter. As an example, if a student pushes the scooter as though he or she were delivering a curling stone, it would probably arrive safely at the intended destination. If a student called out a teammate's name and pushed the scooter directly toward that student, it should also arrive in a responsible manner. On the other hand, if a student carelessly flings the scooter across an open space, it could interfere with another group or strike a student who may not be watching the action. We recommend a clear discussion concerning the responsible transferring of scooters. We have found that students are excited about using scooters, and we have not witnessed accidents, but that favorable circumstance may be because we insist that users follow safety rules and suggestions.

Cage Balls

Another piece of equipment that we regularly use is a large, inflatable cage ball. Generally, we use a 48- or 60-inch (120- or 150-centimeter) diameter ball. The appearance of a large ball of this nature elicits some overwhelming desires. First, students are tempted to run up and kick the ball, an action that in a learning environment might be more disruptive than harmful or dangerous. The second temptation is to run, jump on the ball, and roll over, an exploit that can result in the student landing on his or her head, which is not a safe maneuver or strategy. No matter what activity or lesson you teach, you will eventually find yourself in a situation that you never anticipated. We had a student whose method of moving the cage ball was to hold the laces with his teeth and try to carry it across a long space. To say the least, this way of using the ball is not acceptable, although it may be a clever solution to a challenge.

Poly Spots and Vinyl Bases

Vinyl bases or poly spots are other items that we use in a few challenges. To keep them from moving or slipping out from under the participants' feet, we recommend cutting strips of mat tape, folding the strips over, and placing them underneath the base to create a sticky bond from the base to the floor. Mat tape is usually sold in rolls that are 3 or 4 inches (8 or 10 centimeters) wide. The primary use of mat tape is to repair wrestling or tumbling mats or to tape them together. This type of tape is usually a thick, clear vinyl product. Most sporting-goods catalogs carry this product.

Wooden Boards

Some challenges use wooden boards, such as two-by-fours (boards about 3.8 centimeters thick and 9.0 centimeters wide) that are 8 feet (2.5 meters) long. For participants of any age, we suggest that a discussion take place regarding common sense when transferring equipment. As an example, this discussion could cover the hazard of stepping on one end of a board that is unsupported at the other end. This action could cause the board to flip up and lead to an uncomfortable and embarrassing event. Allowing a board to fall from a vertical position could cause someone to be hurt. Turning quickly while holding a board in a horizontal position could cause the board to hit another person. Covering the edges of the board with duct tape will eliminate the possibility of someone getting a splinter.

Plungers

In some challenges, we use plungers—yes, the old-fashioned rubber toilet plunger. In our challenges, participants use plungers primarily as a pushing device or to manipulate a ball. No matter what the age of your participants, an overwhelming desire develops to place the plunger on another person's head, to stab the plunger to the ground so that the suction cup sticks, or to throw the plunger toward the ceiling to see if it can be stuck there. Discourage all of these incorrect uses; describe or pretend to show the participants in a humorous way what you are thinking. If you do not address the issue right away, you will have some equipment problems. Plungers that are stuck to the ground, for instance, are usually pulled up quickly by the person who jammed the plunger down, possibly causing damage to the threads inside the plunger and reducing its effectiveness as a tool for your challenge.

Tug-of-War Ropes

A few challenges use tug-of-war ropes. These ropes are generally heavy but usually do not pose a great safety risk. Some cheap manila ropes have fibers that break off like tiny slivers; avoid using these ropes. If participants swing a rope in a careless or lasso fashion, they may strike another person and cause an injury.

Blindfolds

We have used blindfolds in a number of our challenges. We have also noted with interest that many of our students and workshop participants like to add handicapping conditions as variations to many of the challenges that we do or that they create. Having teammates give up their sight is usually the first idea presented. Participants who choose to wear the blindfolds need to make a commitment that they will not wander away from the group when blindfolded. Group members can trip on objects or teammates, run into objects, or accidentally strike another person with a piece of equipment during the challenge. Sighted teammates need to monitor their blindfolded team members to ensure their safety.

Safety Issues With Specific Challenges

As we noted earlier, we will include specific safety concerns for each challenge in the book, but some safety issues are important enough to be considered in a general discussion on safety. By highlighting these issues for a few specific challenges, we believe that you will think about safety for every challenge you present to your participants.

Black Hole

In one of the advanced challenges, Black Hole (see chapter 8), we use a hula hoop suspended from a basketball hoop. We recommend attaching the hoop to a jump rope using a piece of masking tape.

If a student should fall or put too much pressure on the hoop during this challenge, the tape will quickly snap, and the hoop will fall. This setup prevents a participant from falling onto the hoop and being suspended on the hoop or crashing to the ground. This circumstance could occur if the hoop is attached directly to the rope. In addition, we recommend that sufficient padding, in the way of crash pads or tumbling mats beneath the hoop, always be in place to break the fall of anyone who loses his or her balance or is dropped by the group.

During this challenge, participants lift their teammates. Remind the group to lift safely and correctly (using their legs). Some students have an overwhelming desire to dive headfirst through the hoop. Do not allow this action to be part of the solution. Other teammates may suggest that the group throw someone through the hoop, or a student may volunteer to be thrown through the hoop; this technique is not safe, either. Make sure that this challenge has a crash pad as a base for proper standing support.

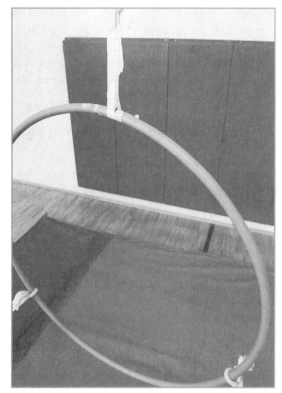

In the Black Hole challenge, the rope should loop over the basketball hoop, and the hanging ends should be tied together. Attaching tape between the hanging rope and the hula hoop will allow it to be suspended.

Electric Fence

Electric Fence (see chapter 8) is an advanced challenge in which participants cross a high balance beam by going under a net that is hanging above and touching the beam. You should consider having participants wear long-sleeve shirts and long pants because they may obtain bruises and burns from attempting to get on the balance beam. Make sure that plenty of mats are on the floor. Keep the balance beam as low as possible while leaving enough room for participants to hang under the beam without touching the floor.

Knights of the Around Table

Knights of the Around Table (see chapter 8) is an advanced challenge that requires the group to transfer all members over and under a table without touching the floor. Do not allow team members to go feet first around the table because doing so puts their heads in an unsafe position. Also, be certain that the table you use is extremely sturdy.

Bridge Over the Raging River

Bridge Over the Raging River (see chapter 7) requires all group members to cross a distance using four automobile tires, two 8-foot-long (2.5-meter-long) boards, and two ropes. Participants must use caution when moving the two-by-four boards. In addition, the group must be aware that a board could flip up if someone steps on one end of the board without having the other end supported. Participants also must be careful when lifting and moving tires.

We hope that this discussion of safety issues for a few challenges will prompt you to think about safety concerns when administering the challenges. The challenges are fun and motivating. Our own students and workshop participants continually challenge us to think about safety. If we do not address safety concerns, someone will find a dangerous way of solving a challenge or circumventing a rule.

Creative Ways to Obtain Equipment

Having been teachers for a combined 90 years, we have spent our careers with limited budgets, living within frugal means, and making the best of whatever equipment we could accumulate. Most teachers understand this all too well. When we began creating team-building challenges, we looked at the equipment and supplies we had in our storerooms and asked, "How can we use what we have, or what we can get?" We were not entrepreneurs looking to manufacture products to sell. We were painfully pragmatic. Collect automobile or trailer tires free of charge from your own home, friends, tire stores, or service stations; you should not have to spend a dime to get decent tires. Remember to clean the tires before using them. Wooden boards used in challenges are available at reasonable prices at any lumber store. If you work for an educational or parochial institution, ask a contractor or carpenter to donate materials and perhaps gain a tax deduction. Buy sash cord rope from a hardware store or full-service lumber store at a reasonable cost. Some items, such as plungers and highway-type cones, can be found in liquidation stores or unclaimed freight stores. Certain items that we use, such as scooters, cage balls, poly spots, vinyl bases, tug-of-war ropes, cones, and deck tennis rings, are available from sporting-goods suppliers such as Gopher Sport of Owatonna, Minnesota.

If you have virtually no money in a budget, you may wonder what you can do to obtain equipment. Here are a few suggestions. If you work in a school, request assistance such as funds or a grant from a parent-teacher organization such as the PTA, PTO, or PTSA. In many communities, organizations that deal with charitable gambling or pull-tabs must donate, by law, a percentage of their earnings to educational or charitable organizations. Contact a group such as your local VFW or Lions Club and inquire about their grant policies. Companies such as General Mills sponsor label and point programs that are designed to exchange product proofs of purchase for athletic or physical education equipment.

We recommend that you buy safety equipment, such as tumbling mats or crash pads, from a reputable company or manufacturer. Likewise, you should buy items such as balance beams, cargo nets, and climbing ropes through a commercial enterprise. Making your own gymnastics equipment could open you up to legal and liability issues.

One of our challenges, Toxic Waste Transfer (see chapter 6), uses a 5-gallon (20-liter) paint bucket or sheetrock joint compound bucket. You should always be able to find this item free of charge. In the bucket, you use packing peanuts, a product that you should also be able to save or find without cost; just ask friends, family, or neighbors to save packing peanuts for you. Poles such as those used in Plunger Ball (see chapter 7) can be found in the plumbing section of any home store. PVC plumbing pipe in 8- or 10-foot (2.5- to 3-meter) sections is inexpensive. We still use thick bamboo poles, which used to be available from carpet companies who used them inside the carpet rolls. If you cannot afford vinyl bases or poly spots, you could use carpet sample pieces; ask a carpet establishment for discontinued samples.

Our intention here is to show you that you do not need a great deal of money to use the challenges we have written or to create your own challenges. When we have conducted team-building classes and have assigned our students the task of creating their own challenges, we often find that they come up with ideas from the equipment that we have on hand or from items that they find in their own homes. An example of this is Great Balls of Color (see chapter 7), a challenge that is now being sold in catalogs. Our challenge designers simply took a twin-size bedsheet, cut five holes, used five different-colored markers to outline the holes, and used five colored softball-sized Whiffle balls to create a challenge that they called Hole in the Bucket. This group created a challenge that cost them nothing except the resources that they found in their own homes. Practical use of existing equipment and materials and a mindset of safety will allow you to create an inventory of team-building supplies.

As team building has become popular over the past number of years, more sporting-goods companies are carrying inventories of the equipment needed for team-building activities and challenges. Many companies are encouraging teachers and instructors to invent new challenges based on creative equipment uses and designs. We will be including some of these challenges in the next few chapters.

Summary

Using good judgment and common sense is no different for team building than for any other physical activity. Be sure that the equipment is safe, that floor areas are properly matted, and that participants understand that horseplay can result in unsafe conditions or injuries.

PART II

TEAM-BUILDING ACTIVITIES AND CHALLENGES

Chapter 5

Icebreakers and Communication Activities

Icebreakers and communication activities are similar because both activities require participants to communicate. These enjoyable and easy activities allow teammates to become more relaxed and comfortable with each other. We usually do three or four icebreakers before we feel a team is ready to move on to the introductory challenges. No set formula tells us how many to do; the instructor should decide when the team is ready to move on. The Great Communicator, Agadoo, Memory Game, and Where Do I Go? foster team unity and help create a relaxed atmosphere. We do these activities before doing any challenges. These activities have no group size restrictions or age restrictions. And, very importantly, they are fun. When people are having fun, especially as a team, they are more engaged and motivated to continue.

For more innovative mixers and warm-ups, see pages 34 through 49 of *Building Character, Community, and a Growth Mindset in Physical Education* (Anderson and Glover 2017).

AGADOO

We use this dance and communication game to break the ice before team building.

Equipment

- The Agadoo song and dance directions (*Children's Party Album,* Pop All-Stars)

Setup

Class members can stand anywhere they choose on half of a basketball court. When the music and singing start, the class must perform the dance. When the dance stops and the chorus starts, class members must high-five and say the name of as many classmates as they can before the dance starts again.

When the chorus starts for the second time, participants must double high-five and greet as many classmates as they can before the dance starts again. The instructor can choose different greetings each time the chorus starts, such as an elbow-to-elbow or knees-to-knees greeting.

Rules and Sacrifices

1. Each classmate must attempt to meet and greet as many people in the class as possible.
2. Classmates must listen to the music while greeting so they are ready for the Agadoo dance.

Conclusion of the Task

When the music is over, the challenge can conclude.

During the chorus, high-five as many people as you can before the verse starts. When the verse starts, repeat the dance.

Additions and Variations

- Use the entire gym. Make the space larger or smaller.
- While greeting classmates, students should learn the names and favorite food of as many people as they can. How many can they remember?

Safety Considerations

If the students are allowed to run and high-five their greetings, caution them about running into classmates.

1. Agadoo-do-do
jab index fingers
forward 3 times

2. Push pineapple
pushing movement
forward with hands

3. Shake tree
clasp hands together swing
over left shoulder and right

4. Agadoo-do-do
jab index fingers
forward 3 times

5. Push pineapple
pushing movement
forward with hands

6. Grind coffee
make circles with hands
over each other
roly-poly movement

7. To the left
point left arm in
the air

8. To the right
point right arm in
the air

9. Jump up
both hands
in the air

10. And down
bring arms down
to knees

11. Cross over
hands at knees

12. Then bring
hands back

During chorus high-five as many people as you can before
verse starts, and when verse starts repeat dance.

Doing the Agadoo dance.

Memory Game

This is an enjoyable icebreaker activity to do before team building.

Equipment

- Any type of music the instructor desires

Setup

The group should be scattered and standing around half of the gym floor. When the music starts, the class starts jogging within the boundaries that the instructor has set. When the music stops, everyone must find a high-five partner. Students give their high-five partners a high five and introduce themselves. When the music starts again (the instructor should wait 5 to 10 seconds), the class resumes jogging. When the music stops again, classmates must find a new person to double high-five and then find and single high-five their original single high-five buddy. When the music resumes (after 10 to 15 seconds), the class starts jogging. The third time the music stops, classmates must find a new elbow-to-elbow partner, find and double high-five their double high-five partner, and find and single high-five their single high-five partner. This sequence can go on and on; it will become harder to remember the sequence of greetings.

Possible greetings include back to back, pinky to pinky, toes to toes, or knees to knees.

Rules and Sacrifices

There are no rules and sacrifices for this icebreaker, but remind the class of the boundaries for this game.

Possible Solutions

The students greet all their greeting buddies in reverse order before the music ends. They must make an effort to remember the order.

Conclusion of the Task

When the students have successfully greeted all their partners in order by the music's end, the task is complete.

Additions and Variations

- Classmates must change the way they move every time the music starts playing.
- Shorten or lengthen the amount of time for the sequence of greetings.

Safety Considerations

This game, like Agadoo, is a very safe and fun activity. However, caution participants to be aware of any others in the space.

MEXICAN HAT ROCK–LA RASPA

This activity is not only a good mixer but also a warm-up.

Equipment

- A sound system and the Mexican Hat Rock music for La Raspa

Setup

The class is spread out in the gym; each classmate should be facing a partner. When the music starts, the partners perform the footwork used in the Mexican Hat Rock dance, also known as La Raspa. When the La Raspa dance is over and the chorus starts, the partners leave each other and move throughout the gym to high-five as many classmates as they can. As soon as the La Raspa steps start again, students must attempt to find a new partner and perform the steps. When the La Raspa steps stop again and the chorus starts, the students attempt to double high-five as many classmates as possible. This series continues until the end of the song.

Rules and Sacrifices

There are no specific rules or sacrifices for this activity; however, encourage the students to try and greet everyone in class.

Conclusion of Task

When the song is over, the Mexican Hat Rock dance is complete.

Additions and Variations

- Make the students move a different way after each La Raspa dance.
- Encourage groups of four instead of two while doing the La Raspa steps.
- Use your imagination to change the way the students greet one another when the chorus is playing.

Safety Considerations

Caution the students and tell them to use their agility to avoid any collisions while moving through the gym.

CHICKEN DANCE

Like La Raspa, this can be used as an icebreaker or a warm-up.

Equipment

- A sound system and the music for the chicken dance (video of dance and music can be found online)

Setup

The class is scattered around one half of the gym facing the instructor and the music. When the music starts, the students perform the chicken dance and do the following steps:

1. Pinch fingers and thumbs together four times with hands at shoulder height.
2. Flap elbows up and down four times.
3. Wiggle body four times while bending knees.
4. Clap four times.
5. Repeat this sequence.
6. When the promenade music starts, high-five as many classmates as you can before the dance moves start again.
7. The next time the promenade music begins, double high-five as many classmates as possible.

Each time the promenade music begins, the students should greet classmates a new way, such as elbows to elbows, knees to knees, and back to back.

Rules and Sacrifices

There are no rules or sacrifices for this challenge. Encourage the students to greet as many other students as possible.

Conclusion of Task

When the music is over, the task is complete.

Additions and Variations

- Make the students move in a different manner each time the series of greetings start.
- Make the space larger or smaller.

Safety Considerations

There are no safety considerations for this icebreaker. Caution the students to use their agility to avoid bumping into classmates.

GROUP CONSTRUCTION

This activity can be quite difficult for younger students, so read the Additions and Variations section to make modifications.

Equipment

- Ten toothpicks for each team member

Setup

Team members sit in a semicircle with their backs to the center of the circle. They should not be able to see other group members' toothpicks as they build their designs on the floor.

One team member is designated as the construction manager and sits with his or her back to the rest of the team on the opposite side of the semicircle. The construction manager places his or her toothpicks on the floor one at a time and attempts to build a design. After placing each toothpick on the floor, the construction manager orally guides the rest of the team to place their toothpicks in the same position. The construction manager tries to get all the builders to construct the same design that he or she is building.

Rules and Sacrifices

1. The construction manager is the only one who can speak.
2. The construction manager must give directions one toothpick at a time.
3. No one may look at the construction manager's design or at any other builder's design before completion.

Group members should not be able to see each other's toothpicks.

4. The construction manager may not look at the builders' designs before completion.

After the construction manager gives the direction for the last toothpick, the builders and the construction manager look at each other's designs. How many designs exactly matched the construction manager's design?

Possible Solutions

The builders must concentrate on the construction manager's explanation. The construction manager should speak slowly and give specific directions.

Conclusion of the Task

When all builders have a completed toothpick design that matches the construction manager's design, the task is complete.

Additions and Variations

- Allow the builders to speak and ask questions of the construction manager.
- Let one student observe and give feedback to the builders based on his or her vision of the design.
- Let the builders work together as one team with 10 toothpicks.
- Add toothpicks.
- After one person has had a chance to be the construction manager, allow another student to attempt the challenge.

Safety Considerations

This game presents no safety considerations.

Moving Team Juggle

This activity is a variation of the cooperative team juggle activity from *The Cooperative Sports and Games Book* by Terry Orlick (1978). The adaptation we have made makes this activity more difficult and interesting.

Equipment

- Three foam balls—either footballs or soccer balls—for each team

Setup

The group stands in a circle. One of the team members holds the three foam balls. When everyone is ready, the person starts tossing the three balls, one at a time, to a team member across the circle. Teammates continue to toss the balls around the circle until everyone has had a chance to catch all three balls. The last person to catch should be the person who started the rotation. Each team member must remember to whom he or she tossed the balls and that person's name.

Rules and Sacrifices

1. If a ball hits the ground, the group must start the process over.
2. The primary purpose while in the circle is to learn the rotation. Before starting the balls around a second time, group members must be moving.
3. The team may not move as a unit. Team members must jog in different directions around the gym while attempting to pass and catch in the same rotation as they did in the circle.

Possible Solutions

Students must be very alert as balls come at them one right after another. Also, students must remember who threw to them and to whom they threw.

Conclusion of the Task

When all three balls have been successfully passed in the correct rotation, the task is complete.

Additions and Variations

- Use fewer balls or use more balls.
- Allow the team to move as a unit.
- At the instructor's signal, team members must change the way they move.
- When several teams attempt this challenge at once, the activity becomes quite difficult.

Safety Considerations

The students are not only moving among their classmates in the gym but also throwing and catching. Caution them to be aware of others and avoid contact.

Adapted from Terry Orlick (1978).

Untying Knots

This is an old activity with a new twist.

Equipment

- Six to eight cloth ropes that are 8 to 10 feet (2.5 to 3 meters) long

Setup

The team stands in a circle about the width of the basketball center circle. Team members must connect to another person in the circle with a rope. They may not connect with a person next to them. One group member (A) holds one end of a rope in his or her right hand and connects with the right hand of a group member across the circle. Person A then connects his or her left hand with the rope to the left hand of a different group member. This process continues until all group members are connected to one other person's right hand and a different person's left hand. The group may need several attempts to link up properly, but this could be part of the puzzle. See the diagram.

Rules and Sacrifices

1. Group members may not let go of their ropes or change hands with the ropes.
2. Group members must communicate and move their bodies and ropes to untie the knot and create a connected circle like the one shown in the diagram. Some group members may be facing outward. That configuration is acceptable as long as the rope and bodies form a circle.

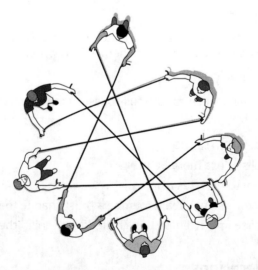

Group members who are standing directly next to one another should not be holding the same rope. The right hand of one group member's rope should lead to the right hand of the group member holding the opposite end of the same rope. The same is true for left hands.

Possible Solutions

The students must cooperate and decide who should move in order to untie the knot. Students may have to duck under or step over other ropes to form the finished circle.

Conclusion of the Task

When the ropes and team members form a connected circle, the task is completed.

Additions and Variations

- Try different lengths of rope.
- The original directions ask participants to reach across the circle and connect hands.

Safety Considerations

This game presents no safety considerations.

Group members must cooperate to figure out who needs to move in order to untie the knot.

Adapted from Terry Orlick (1978).

WHERE DO I GO?

Perform this icebreaker in groups of two. Very specific directions must be given by each group member. Challenge the participants to see if they can accomplish the task in four moves or less.

Equipment

- Two small objects such as toothpicks, coins, or paper clips

Setup

Students are scattered around the gym in groups of two. One team member is blindfolded. (Caution: Make sure that the blindfolded person does not move around without direction from his or her partner.) The sighted partner places two small objects (such as toothpicks) behind the blindfolded person and close enough that the blindfolded person can simultaneously cover each object with each foot. The sighted team member can give one direction, such as, "Turn around 180 degrees" or "Move your left foot forward 6 inches (15 centimeters)." The sighted team member gives directions until the blindfolded person covers the two objects with his or her feet.

Rules and Sacrifices

1. Each sighted group member can give only one direction at a time.
2. The blindfolded person may not speak.

Possible Solutions

The sighted team member must give very clear, concise directions to the blindfolded person.

Conclusion of the Task

The task is complete when the blindfolded person's feet are completely covering both objects.

Additions and Variations

- Partners change roles after a successful attempt.
- Put down four objects and decide which objects should be covered by a hand and which objects should be covered by a foot.

Safety Considerations

The obvious safety concern here is having one team member's eyes covered by a blindfold. Caution that person to move only when told to move by another team member. The entire group must be aware of the insecurity of the blindfolded teammate and look out for his or her welfare.

THE GREAT COMMUNICATOR

The Great Communicator is an effective challenge for building teamwork. Although it is not a physical challenge like the others, it is helps develop listening skills. Group members also need to practice clearly explaining their ideas. You can use The Great Communicator with all your groups at one time. Space is not an issue here. This challenge can be done in a classroom or gymnasium.

Try this challenge early in your team-building program. As your groups develop (or struggle to develop), you may wish to use this challenge from time to time as a test of communication success.

Group members sit either in a semicircle or in a random pattern in an area assigned only to that group. One member of the group is selected as the Great Communicator.

The Great Communicator attempts to describe a picture in terms that allow the group members to draw the objects that he or she is describing, but the Great Communicator may not use certain terms that describe shapes, such as *circle, square, rectangle, triangle,* and *arc.* Group members cannot ask the Great Communicator questions or ask for further descriptions. Give the task of Great Communicator to a different group member after each picture is completed.

Equipment

- Pencils and paper
- A picture to describe (see the diagram for examples or make up your own)
- A clipboard

The Great Communicator should use a clipboard so that teammates cannot see through the page.

Setup

Groups need the necessary equipment and a 10-foot (3-meter) circle or square work space.

Rules and Sacrifices

1. There are no sacrifices in this challenge.
2. The Great Communicator cannot use the designated terms (*square, circle, rectangle, triangle,* and *arc*).

Conclusion of the Task

The task ends when the Great Communicator finishes describing the picture. The group members show their finished drawings to the Great Communicator and to each other.

Additions and Variations

- Feel free to use the picture examples that we have provided.
- Supply your groups with additional or more creative examples to describe.
- Allow students to use all words.

Safety Considerations

This challenge includes no obvious safety considerations.

Describe this picture. You may not use the following words: circle, square, triangle, rectangle, arc.

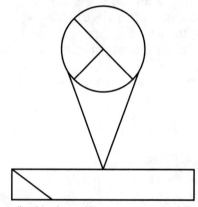

Describe this picture. You may not use the following words: circle, square, triangle, rectangle, arc.

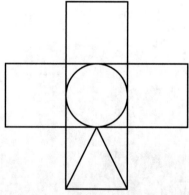

Describe this picture. You may not use the following words: circle, square, triangle, rectangle, arc.

Examples of pictures to describe during The Great Communicator challenge.

BREAK MY STRIDE

This challenge serves as an icebreaker or a warm-up.

Equipment
- Music for "Break My Stride"
- A sound system

Setup
Students are scattered around the gym. When the music starts, the students start moving around the gym as instructed. Some methods of movement include running, walking, galloping, hopping, skipping, etc. When the instructor signals, the students must change the way they are moving. When the "never going to break my stride" chorus begins, the students do jumping jacks to the rhythm of the music. When the "never going to break my stride" chorus is over and the song resumes, the students attempt to greet everyone in class with a high five. The high fives continue until the "never going to break my stride" chorus begins again; the students then do jumping jacks until the chorus is over. When the chorus is over and the song resumes, the students now attempt to greet everyone in class with at least three different greetings (double high-five, elbows to elbows, back to back, knees to knees). This sequence continues until the song is over.

Rules and Sacrifices
There are no rules or sacrifices for this icebreaker. Encourage the students to greet as many classmates in as many different ways as possible.

Conclusion of Task
When the song is over, the task is complete.

Additions and Variations
- Make the space smaller.
- Greet each student in a foreign language; the instructor will need a chart showing some foreign language greetings.

Safety Considerations
Caution the students to use their agility and avoid collisions while moving throughout the gym.

References

Anderson, L., and D. Glover. 2017. *Building Character, Community, and a Growth Mindset in Physical Education* (Champaign, IL: Human Kinetics).

Orlick, T. 1978. *The Cooperative Sports and Games Book: Challenge Without Competition* (New York City: Pantheon).

Chapter 6

Introductory Challenges

"Self-esteem is most likely to be fostered when children have challenging opportunities to build self-confidence and esteem through effort, persistence and the gradual accrual of skills, knowledge and appropriate behavior. Learning to deal with setbacks and maintaining the persistence and optimism necessary for childhood's long and gradual road to mastery: These are the real foundations of lasting self-esteem."

From "All About Me" by Lillian Katz.

In many team situations, the most outgoing, most intelligent, or most athletic people tend to dominate decisions and activities. In team building, everyone has a role, and everyone is a valued member regardless of skill or ability level. The following activities are classified as introductory because they are both physically and intellectually strenuous yet achievable by most groups.

CONSTRUCTION ZONE

Like The Great Communicator (see chapter 5), Construction Zone is more of a communication challenge than it is a physical challenge. Group members attempt to assemble a large puzzle. One set of group members uses verbal clues and cues to assist construction workers, who will be wearing blindfolds. The sighted group members must communicate in a clear manner so that the blindfolded construction workers can follow the directions and complete the puzzle.

You can have as many group members blindfolded as you wish; at least one group member must remain sighted.

For our task discussion, let's assume that three or four group members are blindfolded. After blindfolding the designated group members, the sighted group members mix up the parts of the puzzle. Although your students could create many types of puzzles, assume that the puzzle will become a square when assembled. The sighted group members give verbal directions to the blindfolded members, guiding them to the puzzle pieces and then guiding them to place the pieces in the correct positions. The sighted group members are not allowed to touch the puzzle pieces or the blindfolded group members. Clear the work area of obstructions or other physical structures.

Equipment
- One to four blindfolds
- A construction puzzle (see diagram; the puzzles could be made from a 4-foot square piece of 1/4-inch (60-millimeter) plywood or even tag board)

Setup
This challenge does not require a great deal of space. The task could be done in a classroom, hallway, or gymnasium. A 10-by-10-foot (3-meter-by-3-meter) area with no obstructions is adequate.

Rules and Sacrifices
1. Only blindfolded team members may touch the puzzle pieces. If sighted members touch the puzzle pieces, the group must mix up the puzzle pieces again and start from the beginning.
2. The sighted group members may not touch the blindfolded group members. The same sacrifice as in rule 1 applies.
3. Group members cannot use last names or put-downs.

Possible Solutions
The solution to the task is to assemble the puzzle. The level of difficulty depends on the verbal skills of the sighted group members and the manipulative skills of the blindfolded construction workers. Increase the level of difficulty by providing puzzles that are more difficult.

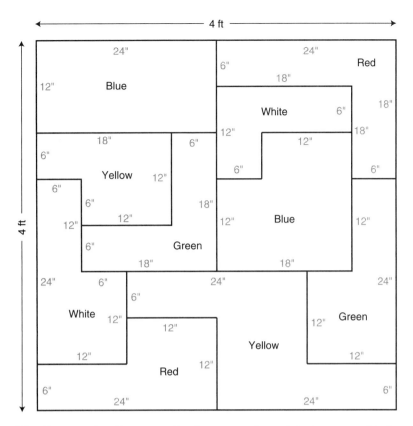

The Construction Zone puzzle pieces can be painted on one side to make the challenge easier for younger participants (not using blindfolds).

Conclusion of the Task

When the group has assembled the puzzle, the blindfolded group members remove their blindfolds.

Additions and Variations

- Put a time limit on each construction group.
- Tape an outline of the puzzle to the floor to help the group in the construction process.
- To give all group members a turn as blindfolded construction workers, have the group rebuild the puzzle with new blindfolded members or provide the group with a new puzzle.
- Using large puzzles seems to be more motivating for both the people involved in the task and those observing the challenge.

Safety Considerations

Blindfolded team members should remain seated. They should not be allowed to wander from the work area or walk around unattended. In addition, blindfolded team members must be careful when handling and passing the puzzle pieces.

GEOGRAPHY MASTERS

This challenge was created after buying a large rubber (poly) map of the United States from a sporting-goods catalog. The procedure for this challenge can be similar to that of Construction Zone or changed by either adding or omitting different forms of communication.

The team attempting this challenge starts with a 50-piece puzzle of the United States either in a box or with the puzzle pieces stacked in a large pile. For the purpose of this description, the challenge will be for the group to assemble the puzzle without using any form of oral communication. Having team members compete against a stopwatch might add value to the challenge.

Equipment

- A large United States puzzle (such as a puzzle like the USA Poly Puzzle sold by Gopher Sport)
- A picture map of the United States (optional)
- Blindfolds for at least half of the group (optional)
- A stopwatch (optional)

Setup

A space about 8 feet (2.5 meters) square should provide enough room for a group to perform the challenge. Place the puzzle pieces in a box or stack the pieces in a pile in the middle of the work space. After the group has read the challenge and organizer cards, they can turn over the box or simply start sifting through the stack of puzzle pieces.

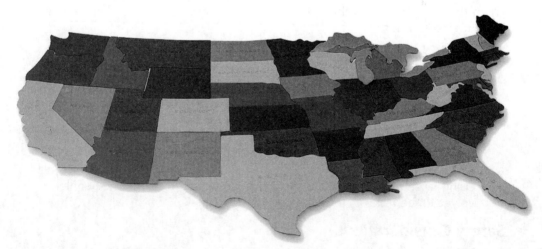

The USA Poly Puzzle includes the Great Lakes as well as the states.

© Gopher Sport

Rules and Sacrifices

1. No one may use any form of oral communication (speaking, throat noises, coughing, or any other sound coming from the mouth or throat).
2. If the group breaks rule 1, it must restack the puzzle pieces and start from the beginning.

Possible Solutions

A puzzle of the United States will be assembled.

Conclusion of the Task

Group members throw their hands in the air when they complete the puzzle. This signal should get the attention of the instructor, who then can stop the stopwatch.

Additions and Variations

- Fourth-grade students can handle this challenge using an outline map of the United States without the names of the states appearing on the map. Consider providing younger children a map of the states with names. Older participants may not need a map at all.
- Provide the map but keep the map 15 or 20 feet (4.5 to 6 meters) away from the group so that group members must run to another place to get clues for putting the puzzle together.
- Create a relay-running adaptation in which group members must run to an area where the puzzle pieces are located, run back with a puzzle piece, give it to an installer, and then send another runner to get an additional piece.
- This task can also use rules similar to those of Construction Zone, in which half of the group is blindfolded. The sighted people may use oral communication, but they may not touch the puzzle pieces or their blindfolded teammates.

Note: If you use an adaptation of this challenge, provide the necessary changes in the rules and sacrifices, the directions on the challenge card, and the questions on the organizer card.

Safety Considerations

If groups do this task with all members sighted, it includes no obvious safety considerations. If some team members are blindfolded, they should remain seated and not wander or walk around unattended.

GENERAL HOSPITAL, EMERGENCY ROOM

This challenge is another group task that can serve as a regular team-building challenge or as a communication activity. The challenge was created after buying a 7-foot (2-meter), 21-piece vinyl skeleton puzzle from a sporting-goods catalog. General Hospital, Emergency Room closely follows the Construction Zone challenge.

Half of the group members are blindfolded, and the other half remain sighted. Group members receive the skeleton puzzle, either in a container or stacked up in a single pile of puzzle pieces. They then construct the skeleton.

Equipment

- A skeleton puzzle either in a container or piled in a single stack of puzzle pieces
- Blindfolds for at least half of the group
- A drawing of the skeleton, depending on the age of the group
- A work area of approximately 8 feet (2.5 meters) square

Setup

Place the puzzle pieces in the work area. Provide enough blindfolds and the skeleton diagram if necessary.

Teams assemble a skeleton puzzle while half are blindfolded.

Rules and Sacrifices

1. Sighted group members may not touch the puzzle pieces.
2. Sighted group members may not touch the blindfolded group members.
3. If group members break either rule, they must mix up the puzzle pieces and start the task from the beginning.

Possible Solutions

The solution is that the puzzle is assembled with all the pieces in the correct places.

Conclusion of the Task

The sighted group members call the instructor to the work area to approve the skeleton construction before the blindfolded group members remove their blindfolds. The blindfolded members may then remove their blindfolds to view their wonderful creation.

Additions and Variations

- Complete this challenge without blindfolds. For this variation, we recommend that you prohibit oral communication.
- Add competition by timing the construction of the skeleton.
- Add to the difficulty by placing the skeleton drawing a distance away from the group so that group members have to run a short distance to consult the picture of the skeleton.

Safety Considerations

As in the two previous challenges, safety considerations are absent if all group members participate as sighted teammates. If some team members are blindfolded, they should remain seated and not be allowed to wander or walk around unattended.

ATOM TRANSFER

In this challenge, group members attempt to transfer a ball resting on one post to another post using ropes that are attached to a metal ring. Team members may only hold on to the handles attached to the ropes. The other ends of the ropes are attached to the metal ring. Sporting-goods companies that market team-building activities sell the equipment as a set. If you cannot find the atom transfer set, it can be easily made. In its initial form, this challenge is good for young children (ages five to eight). For older participants, we recommend using some of the adaptations.

Group members must transfer the atom (ball) from post A to post B. They may manipulate the ball only by holding on to the rope handles. The ball may not touch the floor or any group member.

Equipment

- The atom transfer set, which includes a metal ring with 8 to 10 ropes (with handles) attached to the ring
- A rubber ball about the size of a softball or baseball
- Two stationary posts approximately 3 feet (90 centimeters) high
- Extra equipment as described in the Additions and Variations section

The team must transfer the atom (ball) from one post to another using only the rope handles.
© Gopher Sport

Setup

A space approximately 20 feet (6 meters) long and 15 feet (4.5 meters) wide is necessary to accommodate this challenge. Set a post at each end of this rectangular space. The ring slips over post A at its base. The ropes extend away from the post, and the ball rests on top of it.

Rules and Sacrifices

1. Group members may hold only the handles of the ropes; they may not touch the rope.
2. The ball cannot touch the floor.
3. The ball may not touch a group member.
4. Group members cannot use last names or put-downs.
5. If the group breaks a rule, it must place the ball back on post A after slipping the ring back over the post and placing it on the floor.

Possible Solutions

The ball will be carried to the second stand. All group members should be holding at least one rope handle. The ball will be placed on the stand so the ring slips over the stand.

Conclusion of the Task

After placing the ball on post B, the team must lower the ring and ropes to the floor without dislodging the ball from the post. The team is done when all the rope handles are lying on the floor.

Additions and Variations

- For students older than third grade, do not allow them to speak.
- Require group members to weave their way through obstacles that they cannot touch.

Safety Considerations

This challenge presents no apparent safety considerations. If obstacles are used, care must be taken so that teammates do not trip over obstacles on the floor.

RIVERBOAT

Riverboat is an introductory challenge that requires a group to transport itself across a large, open space. This task generally has one basic solution, but groups usually use the better part of a class period to complete the challenge.

Group members transfer themselves from one end of a basketball-court-sized area to the other end without touching the floor with their bodies.

The group uses two tumbling mats (folded) to create a riverboat. The group must move the mats so that they do not come unfolded. The group must also prevent the mats from crashing to the floor.

Equipment

- Two standard-size tumbling mats
- Two small tires (preferably boat trailer tires)
- Two long jump ropes (or sash cord)

Setup

You need a long, open space the length of a standard basketball court. A wide hallway would also provide adequate work space.

Using mats as a riverboat, the team must transfer themselves from one end of the court to the other without touching the floor.

Rules and Sacrifices

1. If a group member touches the floor with any part of his or her body, the entire group must go back to the starting position.
2. The group must take all the equipment across the river.
3. The mats must remain folded. If the mats (riverboat) fall apart, the entire group returns to the starting position.
4. If a mat crashes to the floor (explodes), the group must start again.
5. Group members cannot use last names or put-downs.

Possible Solutions

Generally, the group places one mat on the floor and then passes the other mat to the front. Group members move to the front mat and then lift, pass, or slide the other mat to the front and transfer themselves to the new front mat in a leapfrog manner.

Often, they use the tires as tugboats to assist in the passing of the tumbling mats. As lifeboats, the tires also offer a less crowded situation on the riverboat. Groups usually tie the jump ropes to the tires to move them more efficiently.

Conclusion of the Task

The group completes the challenge when it has successfully crossed the river with all the equipment.

Additions and Variations

- Make this task more difficult by creating obstacles in the river or requiring the group to perform a portage.
- Create a storm story whereby the group must reach certain points within time limits or risk taking on more baggage (such as additional equipment).

Safety Considerations

Students should be aware that lifting a heavy tumbling mat awkwardly or incorrectly could result in back muscle pain. Students sometimes put their feet in the tires to hop while moving the equipment; in doing so, they could fall forward and injure themselves if they are not prepared to catch themselves.

SWAMP MACHINE

The Swamp Machine challenge requires group members to transport themselves across a defined space using a tumbling mat. The mat must have its Velcro ends attached so that group members can get inside the unit to operate the machine as they would the tracks of a military tank. We will describe this task using a 6-foot-by-12-foot (180-centimeter-by-360-centimeter) UCS mat with 1-foot (30-centimeter) segments (see Additions and Variations for using other mats).

Group members begin on one side of the gym at a designated island or land space (two unfolded tumbling mats, side by side). Two, three, or four group members get into the swamp machine and maneuver it across the swamp to the other island or land space. Some of the group members then get out of the swamp machine. At least two group members must remain in the swamp machine as it travels back across the swamp to pick up more group members. Group members trade places often because two, three, or four members must always be in the machine as it travels back and forth across the swamp. No group member may take more than two consecutive trips across the swamp. The group continues the challenge until all members have successfully crossed the swamp to the second land space.

Equipment

- Four standard tumbling mats to create two land spaces (two mats, side by side, for each land space)
- A 6-foot-by-12-foot (180-centimeter-by-360-centimeter) UCS tumbling mat with 1-foot (30-centimeter) segments (most standard mats are made in 2-foot [60-centimeter] segments) with Velcro ends that attach together for the swamp machine

Setup

Place two standard tumbling mats, unfolded, side by side to create a land space. Place the other two mats in a similar fashion 30 to 40 feet (9 to 12 meters) away to create a second land space (about half the length of a basketball court or the entire width of the court). Alternatively, any long, open space such as a hallway or cafeteria would be sufficient for this challenge. Place the swamp machine on the first land space with the Velcro ends attached.

Rules and Sacrifices

1. If a group member touches the floor (swamp), that person and one successful person must go back to the first land space.
2. If the swamp machine falls apart, no sacrifice is required if the group members in the swamp machine repair it while it is in the swamp. If the group members in the swamp machine cannot repair it while it is in the swamp, the entire group must return to the first land space.

3. No group member may take more than two consecutive trips across the swamp. If a group member does so, that person and one person from the second land space must go back to the first land space.

4. Two, three, or four group members must always be in the swamp machine as it crosses the swamp. If one or more than four members occupy the swamp machine, the entire group must start the challenge from the beginning.

5. Group members cannot use last names or put-downs.

Possible Solutions

Generally, group members get inside the swamp machine and roll it forward to the other land space. One or two group members get out of the machine, stand on the second land space, and send the machine back to the starting area. The swamp machine may veer off to the side if group members try to go too fast or do not work together carefully. As the swamp machine goes back and forth, group members must make sure that the Velcro ends stay together. They should check the ends after each trip.

Group members need to determine some of their sequences mathematically so that they do not leave teammates stranded near the completion of the challenge. Group members may reach the second land space thinking that they have completed the task only to find that they need to get back into the machine to retrieve additional teammates.

Conclusion of the Task

To conclude the task, all group members will be standing on the second land space with the swamp machine safely parked on shore.

Generally, group members get inside the swamp machine and roll it forward.

Additions and Variations

- Create a story sequence by saying, "A storm is approaching. You have 10 minutes to get your group to safety on the other shore."
- Challenge the group to get their teammates across the swamp in less than four moves.
- If you do not have a mat as we described (a 1-foot segmented mat such as those manufactured by UCS), attach standard tumbling mats together. Make sure that the Velcro ends hold together well.

Safety Considerations

If group members are claustrophobic, suggest that they work near the outside edge in the swamp machine. They will have access to the outside air and will not feel quite as enclosed. Caution group members that their shirts might creep up on them when they are moving inside the machine; suggest that they tuck their shirts into their pants so that no embarrassing moments occur.

When moving the swamp machine, participants may incur injury if they choose to do fast or uncontrolled forward rolls while inside it. While doing forward rolls, team members could fall into one another or could injure their heads or necks by rolling improperly. In addition, suggest that team members remove items from their pockets when participating in this challenge.

THE WHOLE WORLD IN THEIR HANDS

This challenge offers several solutions. A group can solve this challenge quickly if teammates work well together (and have some good luck); the challenge can also be difficult to master. This task requires group members to move or use body parts in ways quite different from those that they use to solve other challenges.

The group tries to transfer a large cage ball, 48 inches (120 centimeters) in diameter or larger, from one end of a gymnasium to the other, a distance of 45 to 60 feet (14 to 18 meters). The larger the ball, the more interesting the challenge. The cage ball starts out resting on an automobile tire. The goal is to move the ball to a second tire at the other end of the gym. The group has to move the ball without letting it touch the floor and without any group member touching it with their hands or arms. The group moves the ball from tire to tire four times. Each trip involves moving the ball in a new manner.

Equipment
- Two automobile tires or two small boxes, big enough to hold the ball so it doesn't roll off
- One large cage ball, 48 inches (120 centimeters) in diameter or larger, or a large Earth ball (commercially sold), inflated to its maximum size

A variety of cage balls.

© Gopher Sport

Setup

Choose an open work space. In addition, the large ball is easier to control away from walls.

Group members start by standing around the cage ball. During the challenge, they may move to other positions.

Rules and Sacrifices

1. The cage ball cannot touch the floor.
2. Group members cannot touch the cage ball with their hands or arms.
3. If the group breaks a rule, it must return the ball to tire 1 and begin the task again.
4. Group members cannot use last names or put-downs.
5. The group must successfully move the ball four times.

Possible Solutions

We've found multiple solutions to this challenge, and undoubtedly you and your students will find others. We offer the following four solutions:

1. Group members lift the cage ball off tire 1 with their feet and crab walk or slide across the gymnasium floor; they use their feet, legs, and upper bodies to keep the ball from rolling over group members and onto the floor. When team members get the cage ball to tire 2, they lift the ball onto the tire, again using all body parts except their hands and arms.
2. Group members lie in two lines similar to railroad tracks. Two group members roll the ball down the lines of bodies, using their bodies to keep the ball from rolling onto the floor. As the cage ball moves, the people on the floor change their positions to lengthen the lines. When the cage ball approaches tire 2, at least four group members should be in position to help get the ball onto the tire.
3. Group members also lie on the floor in this solution, but this time they lie side by side like railroad ties. Again, at least two group members guide the ball across the bodies of their teammates, and group members adjust their positions after the ball crosses them to extend the line.
4. Team members stand with their backs to the ball while one or two group members try to raise the ball high enough with their legs so that their teammates can press against the ball with their backs. The group then tries to walk the ball to tire 2. The teammates who raised the ball with their legs quickly join the group to help control the ball.

Conclusion of the Task

The group achieves success when it rests the cage ball on tire 2 after the fourth attempt.

Additions and Variations

- If students were successful lifting and carrying three different ways, then challenge them for their fourth attempt by saying, "For your last attempt, you may not lift or carry the ball in any way." (Students must now make train tracks with their bodies, and the ball is rolled on the human tracks to its final destination.)

- Consider allowing younger students limited use of their hands or arms.
- To encourage students to think for themselves, you may want to require a group to find a solution different from another group's solution.
- Asking students to move the ball from the end back to the starting tire, using either the first solution or a different method, is a task that requires participation by everyone in the group.

Safety Considerations

Do not allow students to jump on the ball because they could roll over the top of it and land precariously on the floor. We have seen participants attempt to lift the ball by using their teeth to hold the laces of the ball, which is neither wise nor safe. If a team loses control of the ball, team members may, to regain control, run into or chase the ball through the work area of another group; discourage the occurrence of this type of event. Caution group members not to try to keep the ball up by heading it (as they might in soccer). The weight of the large ball could hurt the neck or cause a head injury.

THE SNAKE

The Snake is a shape-building challenge in which groups use a tug-of-war rope as the material to create the desired shapes. After group members create a shape with the rope, they cover the rope with their bodies. This challenge is an easy one to solve, but groups need time to create the number of shapes assigned.

Group members begin this challenge using either a large, open space or a floor space covered by tumbling mats or carpeting. The coiled tug-of-war rope is placed in the middle of the work space. The teacher gives the group a list of shapes, or the group may negotiate with the teacher to build other shapes. We suggest that the groups each make eight different shapes such as numbers, letters, names, words, or designs.

Equipment

- One tug-of-war rope

Setup

All you need is a large, open space, although you may wish to cover the floor with tumbling mats. Place the tug-of-war rope in the center of the work space. Curl the rope into a coil.

Rules and Sacrifices

1. Make the shape using a rope.
2. All group members must lie on or cover the rope.
3. Group members must completely cover the rope.
4. The teacher must approve each shape before the group begins to form another.
5. Group members cannot use last names or put-downs.

This challenge includes no sacrifices, but you should require group members to form clearly identifiable shapes to gain approval.

Possible Solutions

Group members find certain shapes, letters, or numbers easy to build. You may wish to include some easy, moderate, and difficult shapes in the assignment. Younger students can make shapes such as a circle, square, or triangle. Older children can make more difficult objects such as numbers or letters. Teams can do a math problem, and the object they form should be the answer. Group members may find that the rope is longer than the combined lengths of their bodies. They may need some time to discern that they can double the rope if necessary.

All group members must lie on or cover the rope.

Conclusion of the Task

The group solves the challenge when it forms the designated number of assigned shapes. The group should leave the rope in a neat coil at the center of the work area for the next group.

Additions and Variations

- If a tug-of-war rope is unavailable, substitute jump ropes tied together or a clothesline rope 40 to 50 feet (12 to 15 meters) long. You could also use electrical cords 50 to 100 feet (15 to 30 meters) long.
- If simple or familiar shapes are used, add time limits to each task, and award points for reaching certain goals or have groups compete in a timed activity.
- Combine groups and create extra-large projects. Displaying pictures of a successful group making its shapes motivates students.

Safety Considerations

Remind group members not to step on one another when finding their places.

GET A GRIP

This challenge is similar to The Snake in that shapes have to be made with the rope and covered with the team's body parts, but movement has been added. Both The Snake and Get a Grip are excellent challenges for grades K–12 due to the adaptability of the included shapes.

Equipment

- One 16-foot long cloth rope for each team
- A list of eight shapes or math problems (for math problems, groups use the rope to create the answer to the problem)

Setup

Give each team a rope. Groups must then space themselves evenly along the rope with one hand on the rope. The first teammate holds the rope with the left hand and the next teammate on the opposite side of the rope holds it with his or her right hand. When everyone has a grip, they should all face the desired direction of travel. When the instructor gives the predetermined signal (musical cues, shouting a signal, or clapping), the team must move around the gym while holding on to the rope. Each time the teacher give the signal, the team members must change the way they are moving. Some suggested ways to move are run, gallop, skip, or slide. When the music stops or the teacher yells, "Ready," the group stops and gets ready to use the rope to make the shape given by the instructor. Here are some examples of what the instructor can use for shape problems:

- Make a square and cover it completely with your bodies.
- Make a triangle and cover it completely with your bodies.
- Make a circle and cover it with your bodies, but two team members must be standing on the rope and covering it with their feet.
- Solve this equation: $5 + 4 - 3$. Make the sum of that problem; two team members must cover the rope with their feet, and only two can sit on the rope.
- Solve for x: $5x + 5 = 15$. Everyone must cover the rope a different way.

After each team solves the shape problem, groups start moving around the gym again as they wait for a new shape problem.

Rules and Sacrifices

1. Everyone must keep a grip on the rope while moving.
2. Team members may let go of the rope to build their shape.
3. The team must solve the problem correctly as stated by the instructor.
4. Group members cannot use last names or put-downs.
5. If a shape problem is not solved correctly, the instructor may request that the group do it again.

Possible Solutions

The students must listen to the instructor's shape problem and then communicate to solve the problem. When the team members have made the correct shape, they have solved the problem.

Conclusion of the Task

When all shape challenges have been solved correctly, the task is over.

Additions and Variations

- Students must make the shape, and the rope may never touch the ground. Using this variation, the students do not have to cover the shape with their bodies, or they can put the rope on the floor after making the shape in the air.
- Try making a word such as "cat" or "dog" instead of a shape.
- Lengthen the movement time between shapes to increase the physical demand of the challenge.
- Let the students come up with their own shape and have the other teams figure out what the shape is.
- While moving throughout the gym, challenge the teams to "flow" from one locomotor movement to another without stopping.

Safety Considerations

Caution the teams not to run into other teams as they move around the gym. Do not allow students to put the rope around their neck while making shapes.

POWER OF SIX

This challenge allows the teams to create different balance statues while connected. In addition, the teams are allowed to have a certain number of body parts touch the ground while making their connected statue. The teams must also incorporate some part of the environment into their statue and be connected with the selected object as well.

Equipment

No equipment needs to be provided for this challenge. However, if the challenge is done outside, it would be nice to have trees, bushes, rocks, playground equipment, and fences in the area so teams can use them in their statues.

Setup

This challenge can be done outside. The teams should scatter around the work area. The instructor says, "Teams, I want you to make a balance statue; all team members must be connected when the statue is finished. You must use some object in the immediate school vicinity in your statue. Only 12 body parts may touch the ground when the statue is finished."

When the team has completed this task, the instructor says, "Now only 11 body parts can touch the ground, and you still must be connected and use the same object." Upon completion, only 10 body parts can touch the ground. After completion of the statue with 10 body parts touching the ground, the teams must try to flow from 12 body supports to 11 body supports to 10 body supports without becoming disconnected or losing their balance. Challenge cards can be used for this challenge. The instructor must accept each statue before another is built.

Rules and Sacrifices

- Only the required number of body parts can touch the ground.
- If the statue (team) loses its balance and becomes disconnected, the team must start over.
- The object chosen by the team to be part of the statue must be approved by the instructor.
- Group members cannot use last names or put-downs.
- The team members must stay connected while they flow from one balance statue to another.

Possible Solutions

The team members must communicate and agree on what object they will use to help form the statue. The team members must also agree on the shape of the statue and how everyone will be connected. Finally, everyone on the team must help each other to balance.

Conclusion of the Task

The task is over when the team can flow from one balance statue to another without disconnecting.

Additions and Variations

- Encourage teams to stretch their arms, legs, and fingers that are not used in the balance. Make it a beautiful statue.
- Reduce the number of body parts touching the ground but be careful of using too few as it could put a lot of weight on one person.
- Increase the number of body parts touching the ground. Can teams make a statue with 15 body parts touching the ground but only use 8 feet?
- Incorporate more objects into the design.
- Take pictures of the statues and post them in the gym.

Safety Considerations

Teams should not use too few supports; this could put a lot of stress on one body part. Students should not stand or sit on one another's shoulders. Teams should not climb on the chosen objects. Encourage the students to help one another balance.

Created by Victoria Otto, Holistic Mechanics, INC.

TIRE BRIDGE

Tire Bridge is another challenge in which a group moves from one end of a large space, such as a gymnasium, to the other. The group uses automobile tires to construct a moving bridge to cross a river. This task is time consuming but not difficult.

Equipment

- One tire per group member and one additional tire
- Starting and finish lines (usually the boundary lines of a basketball court)

Note: Large tires are harder to move and therefore create work that is more physical. Small tires, such as boat trailer tires, are easier to move, but they may be harder to balance on. Clean the tires before use. Bias-ply tires, difficult to find these days, are less likely to have problems such as exposed belts or threads.

Setup

Place the tires near the starting position (land). If you are using a basketball court or similar space, provide a clear path. The ending position should have enough space so that students can stand "on land" and stack the tires in a column there as well.

Groups use tires to construct a moving bridge.

Because this task is not physically difficult, group members need to encourage one another to concentrate. Groups who do not concentrate may break rules 3 and 4, which follow.

Rules and Sacrifices

1. The students must begin standing on land.
2. Only one person may be on a tire at a time.
3. If any group member touches the river (the floor) with any part of his or her body, the group must move the bridge back to the starting position.
4. If two people step on one tire at the same time, the group must move the bridge back to the start.
5. Group members cannot use last names or put-downs.

Possible Solutions

As they step on the tires and form a line with the tires, group members pass the last tire to the front of the line and, one by one, step forward. Some groups carefully place the tires on the floor ahead; daring groups may toss the tires forward. If group members do not coordinate their moves, someone may step on an occupied tire, requiring the group to start over.

A group may lose control of a tire. A student can place both feet inside the tire and jump toward the runaway tire, but it would be difficult and tiring for the entire group to travel across the river this way.

Conclusion of the Task

The group achieves success when group members have crossed the river and have stacked the tires vertically. Group members cannot step into the river. After the instructor approves a group's accomplishment, have members carry the tires back to the starting position.

Additions and Variations

- Give the group more tires to pass. This variation requires a greater amount of physical labor.
- Place a time limit (such as 20 minutes) on completing the task.

Success!

- Create a zigzag path rather than a straight line.
- Provide islands for resting or regrouping.

Safety Considerations

As with any challenge that uses tires, make certain that the tires have no exposed steel belts that can cause cuts, scratches, or puncture wounds. If you are using large tires, instruct participants to lift the tires properly so that they do not strain their back muscles. Prepare participants to look out for one another so that they can help balance teammates if they should lose their balance. An injury could occur if someone falls awkwardly off a tire onto the floor.

TOXIC WASTE TRANSFER

The Toxic Waste Transfer challenge requires the group to transport an object across an open space without directly touching the object. The group manipulates a bucket filled with small objects using ropes attached to the bucket.

Group members form a circle around a 5-gallon (20-liter) bucket. The bucket has numerous ropes attached to it, and group members hold on to the end of the ropes. Working together, group members transport the bucket from one terminal to the other terminal by manipulating the ropes. The group transfers the contents of the first bucket into the second bucket using the ropes.

Equipment

- A toxic waste transfer bucket
- A second bucket or box for the disposal container
- Two distinct boundaries for the two containers, such as two tumbling mats, hoops, or bicycle tires
- Colored tape to mark the area of the rope that students can handle (for example, mark the end of the rope with green tape and place a piece of red tape 12 inches from the end; students may hold the rope only between the tape lines)
- Packing peanuts, golf balls, or plastic golf balls to fill the toxic waste container

Note: Construct a transfer bucket by using 10 to 12 ropes attached to a 5-gallon (20-liter) pail; the ropes should be at least 10 feet (3 meters) long. Drill holes into the bucket, slip the rope through, and tie a tight knot in the end of the rope (see diagram).

Setup

Place the container with ropes and toxic waste material on the floor approximately 40 to 50 feet (12 to 15 meters) from the second container. A distance of three-fourths of a gym space would be adequate. Use a shorter distance for younger groups if necessary.

Toxic waste transfer bucket.

Rules and Sacrifices

1. If the toxic waste bucket touches the floor, the entire group must start the task from the beginning.
2. If a rope touches the floor, the group starts again.
3. If the toxic waste expert places the spilled contents into the wrong container, the group must go back to the starting point.
4. No one may touch the rope between the red tape mark and the container.
5. Group members cannot use last names or put-downs.

Possible Solutions

One basic solution meets this challenge. Group members carefully transport the contents of the toxic waste container by moving together and manipulating the ropes. As they transfer the contents of the first container into the second, they must work slowly and carefully. If a toxic waste spill occurs, the group must be careful not to let the first container touch the floor.

Conclusion of the Task

The group completes the task when it has transferred all the contents of the first container into the second container without leaving any of the material on the floor.

Additions and Variations

- Allow groups to rest the first container on the floor in designated areas (such as inside hula hoops or bicycle tires) if the group needs to reorganize itself or wait for the toxic waste expert to clean up.
- Allow younger children to hold the rope much closer to the bucket. For example, put colored tape 3 feet away from the bucket for second graders.
- To make the challenge more difficult, require the toxic waste expert to wear protective clothing to clean up the spill (see video in the web resource).

Safety Considerations

Participants could fall if they walk backward and trip over an object lying on the floor.

THE ROCK

Although it appears simple, The Rock challenge requires the group to balance for a specified amount of time on an object (the rock). The object used as the rock determines the difficulty of this challenge.

All group members must balance on the rock (or be off the floor) for a slow count of "one-and-two-and three-and-four-and-five." Group members need to find a way to help each other maintain balance, which means that they may experience close encounters with one another.

Equipment

- A rock (a 13-inch [33-centimeter] automobile tire or a heavy-duty box)
- Several tumbling mats to place under the rock

Note: The size of the tire used in this challenge can make a significant difference in difficulty, so issue smaller tires for smaller-sized groups. A large group (such as 10 group members) may need a 14- or 15-inch (36- or 38-centimeter) tire.

Setup

This task does not require much setup, but you should place the tumbling mat far enough away from walls or other objects so that should a student fall, chance of injury is reduced. The mat should be unfolded. We suggest using three 5-foot-by-10-foot (150-centimeter-by-300-centimeter) mats. Place the rock (tire or box) in the center of the mats.

At first, most groups believe that this task is too easy. However, success does not always come quickly. Because this task requires students to hold on to one another closely, some students will debate whether death is more desirable than touching someone of the opposite sex. Others will love the close encounter.

Rules and Sacrifices

1. All group members must be off the floor (tumbling mat) and on the rock.

2. All group members do not have to be touching the rock as long as they are off the floor.

Teammates must cooperate to help each other balance on the rock.

3. Once a group member has been on the rock, touching the floor (or mat) for even an instant means that the group must start over with no one on the rock.

4. Group members cannot use last names or put-downs.

Note that the mats are considered part of the floor space. If a group member gets off the floor or mat and then steps back down onto the floor or mat, the group starts over.

The group needs to practice until group members are confident that they will succeed when they call the instructor to witness the solution.

Possible Solutions

Most groups fail at first. Group members step onto the rock, hold on to one another tightly, start counting to five, and fall off. After a few such failures, group members learn that they must plan to step onto the rock and hold on to others while maintaining balance. One method is for each group member to hold on to someone directly across from him or her on the rock. As more group members get onto the rock, balancing becomes more difficult. Some groups try to have everyone put one foot on the rock and then all add the second foot on the count of three. Some group members may try to stand in the middle of the rock and have others surround them. Alternatively, a group may try to have its members lie horizontally on the rock and on top of one another. Another group might try having some members sit on teammates' shoulders as they step onto the rock. Discourage this last solution because it is unsafe.

As groups practice, remind them that rule 3 is very specific. A student may start to fall, barely touch the mat, and pop back onto the rock. If anyone touches the mat even for an instant, all group members must get off the rock and start over.

Some students, especially those in upper-elementary grades, may find touching one another difficult. Tell them that they cannot complete the task without physically helping one another. By reinforcing positive group behavior, you help students find satisfaction when they work well together.

Conclusion of the Task

When group members have practiced their solution and are confident that they can succeed, they should call the instructor to the work area. The instructor begins the slow count of five when all group members' feet are off the floor. Although the actual conclusion takes only five seconds, the cheering lasts far longer.

Additions and Variations

- To vary this challenge, lengthen the time limit.
- Use a smaller tire, such as an 11- to 12-inch (28- to 30-centimeter) boat trailer tire.

A 13-inch (33-centimeter) tire works well as a rock. A variation that adds difficulty is to consider the hole in the tire part of the floor. To compensate, let students place their feet inside the tire without touching the floor. To ease the challenge for a large group or a group having considerable difficulty, count the center of the tire as part of the rock.

Safety Considerations

Choosing a good solution usually means that no one will be put into a risky situation. Group members sometimes fall as a group when trying to balance on the tire. This event usually occurs because the group is laughing and being silly. Caution group members that they could be hurt if they fall onto one another carelessly. Make certain that enough mats cover the work area. Occasionally, a group has one group member lie on the tire and then builds a tower of teammates by stacking themselves one on top of another. Although there will be some laughter at first, the people on the bottom will eventually feel the pain of the group. At times like this, a teacher must step in and insist on better behavior. The teacher could do this privately or with a specific group if its members are not working safely.

RIVER CROSSING

River Crossing is a physical challenge that requires a group to cross a designated space. In this task, the group travels across a river that is half the length of a gymnasium or basketball court using two scooters, two deck tennis rings, and a long jump rope.

All group members must get from the clearly marked beginning shore or land area across the river to the opposite shore. They must use the designated equipment when crossing the river, and they cannot touch the river with any part of their bodies. All floor space between the shores is considered part of the river.

Equipment

- Two sitting scooters
- Two deck tennis rings
- One long jump rope (a 14- to 16-foot [4.3- to 4.9-meter] sash cord jump rope works best)
- Starting and finish lines (tape lines or the end boundary and midcourt lines of a basketball court)

Setup

The starting and finish lines should be clearly marked, and the equipment should be lying at the starting line. Set one deck tennis ring on each scooter. Fold the jump rope and lay it across the two scooters. Although this challenge can be done in half a gymnasium space, a wide work area is helpful, such as half the width and half the length of a basketball court.

Team members travel across the river using the scooters. They can use the rope to pull a team member on a scooter. They can use the deck tennis rings to help propel the scooters or tie the rings to the rope to create a pulling device. Students usually try to give their teammates a push start on the scooters to get them partway across the river, but they must avoid pushing so hard that teammates fall forward.

Rules and Sacrifices

1. The river is the entire area between the designated lines.
2. If any part of a person's body touches the river (floor), that person and another who has successfully crossed the river must be sacrificed; those two must start over.
3. The first person across the river cannot be sacrificed. The group can keep one person across the river for the remainder of the challenge.
4. Although the group cannot sacrifice the first teammate who successfully crosses the river, that person cannot touch the river. If that happens, the team must sacrifice a teammate who later crosses successfully in place of the first person.

5. If a person touches the river while trying to rescue equipment, a sacrifice is required.
6. Group members cannot use last names or put-downs.

Possible Solutions

A common solution to this challenge is for one person to go partway across the river on a scooter and then use one or two deck tennis rings to push the rest of the way across. The first person tries to push the scooter back across the river and rolls the deck tennis ring back to the waiting group. If the first person did not take the jump rope across, group members throw the rope to the first teammate safely over the river. Those who successfully cross the river can then throw out the jump rope as a lifeline to pull other group members across.

Conclusion of the Task

To solve the task, all group members and all designated equipment must be across the river at the finish line.

Additions and Variations

- If the width of the river is greater than 35 or 40 feet (11 or 12 meters), you may wish to use two long ropes or one long rope and one short rope. If the width is less than 35 feet (11 meters), two long ropes make the task too easy. Make sure that the combined length of the ropes is shorter than the width of the river.
- To make the challenge more difficult, add obstacles in the river. These obstacles could create path diversions, or they could require sacrifices if touched.
- You could also require group members to carry an object such as a stuffed animal with them, or you could require the group to return safely across the river to the starting line.
- A group may want to use the deck tennis rings as skates. If you do not want them to use the rings in this manner, specify that in the list of rules.

Safety Considerations

When group members transfer scooters across a space, they must take care so that an errant scooter doesn't strike anyone. In addition, if a team decides to push someone on a scooter, team members must take care so that the person does not fall face-first onto the floor.

When returning equipment to the starting area, group members must take care not to hit others with it. For example, a teammate should not throw an empty scooter across the river. The rope is intended to be used as a transferring device, not as a tightrope. When group members attempt to walk across the rope, they cannot help but touch the floor with their shoes.

LIFELINE

Lifeline has become one of our standards when presenting challenges. The basic solution to this challenge includes several variations. The task requires the group to travel about three-fourths the length of a basketball court using two scooters and a tug-of-war rope.

Group members begin at one side of the swamp with only one scooter. Another scooter rests on a tire halfway across the swamp. A tug-of-war rope lies just beyond the end line, on the other side of the swamp. The tire in the middle is an island; therefore, it is not movable. Group members must cross the swamp to retrieve the second scooter and the tug-of-war rope so that they have enough equipment to get all group members across to the other side. Although this challenge has a basic solution, groups will use the equipment in different ways.

Equipment

- Two 12-inch (30-centimeter) scooters or two 16-inch (40-centimeter) scooters for older students, adults, or participants with special needs
- One automobile tire
- A tug-of-war rope 50 to 75 feet (15 to 23 meters) long that will reach across the swamp

Groups will use the equipment in different ways during the Lifeline challenge, but there is one basic solution.

Setup

Set one scooter upside down (so that no one steps on it) just behind the starting line. Set an automobile tire halfway across the swamp. Set a second scooter upside down on the tire. Place the tug-of-war rope across the end line. Have the rope coiled so that the group does not have to untangle it. Make sure that the rope stretches all the way across the swamp area.

Rules and Sacrifices

1. No one may touch the floor with any part of his or her body or clothing.

2. No one may stand on a scooter.

3. If a person breaks a rule, that person and a successful teammate (or the teammate who has advanced the farthest) must go back to the starting line. They may not take a scooter back with them unless it was the first scooter that the group used.

4. Group members cannot use last names or put-downs.

Possible Solutions

A common solution to this task is to send one team member to the tire on one scooter. This person usually gets onto the island and sends the two scooters back to the team. Another team member then goes to the island and, with the help of the person on the island, goes across to the side with the tug-of-war rope. These methods of travel usually include pushing the person on the scooter and that person doing some wiggling or air swimming to propel himself or herself forward. Once a team member reaches the tug-of-war rope, the easiest way to succeed is to string the rope across the swamp so that succeeding team members can pull themselves to the other side. Often the team member on the tire helps stabilize the rope for safe and fast travel. If groups use two scooters for each person, the process often goes faster. Rarely, however, do teams use the scooters in this fashion. Teams will more likely send one scooter for each person.

Elementary-aged students often use a solution in which they get the rope across to the tire and then pull each group member across to the ending side. This method tends to take longer, and the groups usually work extremely hard to repeatedly transfer the rope back to the tire.

Conclusion of the Task

The group completes the task when the entire group has successfully crossed the swamp without touching the floor. Group members need not have all the equipment with them, although they usually do.

Additions and Variations

- Use a 16-inch (40-centimeter) scooter rather than a 12-inch (30-centimeter) scooter for students with special needs.

- Tape two scooters together for a student who cannot fit on one scooter because of an ambulatory problem.

Safety Considerations

Team members need to take care if they choose to push a teammate on the scooter. Remind participants that they need to keep their fingers away from the wheels.

When transferring the scooters from one side of the swamp to the island or to the starting area, students need to push the scooters carefully, not throw them carelessly across the work area. In addition, team members need to show care when trying to get the tug-of-war rope across an open area. A team member who throws the rope in an unsafe manner could hit a teammate with it. Do not allow participants to stand on scooters even if they are accomplished skateboarders.

Magic Bases

A physical educator, Jimmy Gehm, in Missouri gave us this challenge. Although this is considered an introductory challenge, a few minor adjustments to the spacing of the equipment can make it much more difficult. One of the unique elements of this challenge is that group members must maintain a hand-holding arrangement throughout the entire challenge.

During this challenge, teammates must hold hands as they travel through a figure-eight pattern, with one loop open, of 12-inch (30-centimeter) poly spots. Team members may step on the poly spots only after they enter the path. They may not touch the floor or speak to one another during the journey. Group members may touch the floor when they step off the exit base, but they may not release their hands from their teammates.

Equipment

- At least one 12-inch (30-centimeter) poly spot, 12-inch (30-centimeter) square vinyl base, or base made from carpet squares for each group member

Teammates hold hands as they travel through a figure-eight pattern.

Setup

Set up the bases in a figure-eight pattern, with one loop open. Designate one base as the starting base and select another as the exit base. Set the bases a big step apart. The age of the participants plays a role in the distance. The distance between bases should not exceed 2 feet (60 centimeters).

Rules and Sacrifices

1. The team must travel the figure-eight pattern with members holding hands. Hands may not come apart.
2. Team members may not touch the floor between the entry base and the exit base.
3. No more than four feet may be on one poly spot at a time.
4. Group members cannot use last names or put-downs.
5. If a rule is broken, the entire group must start the task from the beginning.

Possible Solutions

The team must proceed slowly, and team members must help one another balance on the bases. A student who hops or jumps to a new base could pull a teammate with whom he or she is holding hands off balance. When team members meet at the crossroad or intersection of the figure eight, they have to communicate nonverbally about how they will pass by their teammates. Teammates may have to hold their arms low so that the lead person can step over them, or they may have to raise their arms so that others may cross beneath their connected arms. Team members have to take turns passing under or over their teammates at the intersection of the path.

Conclusion of the Task

The group masters the challenge when all team members have successfully traveled the figure-eight pattern of bases without touching the floor or becoming disconnected.

Additions and Variations

- Once a teammate steps on a base, he or she may speak. Group members may not speak until they reach the first base. This variation allows group members to offer suggestions during the challenge.
- Give the team a time limit or time the challenge so that the team can compare its time with that of other groups.
- No more than two feet may touch a base. This makes the challenge more difficult.
- Spacing the bases closer together or farther apart can significantly alter the difficulty of this challenge.
- After the first person in line reaches the fifth base, the team must figure out how to have that person become the last one off the path.
- Alternate the direction that each person faces as group members line up to hold hands.

Safety Considerations

Put floor tape on the bottom of the poly spots or bases to prevent them from slipping. Caution group members to let go of teammates' hands if they lose their balance and cannot regain it. Starting the challenge over is better than causing team members to fall on top of one another.

LET'S BUILD TOGETHER

This is a great communication challenge for both listening and speaking. The team must work together to build a design that is provided by the teacher. The team must build the design out of buckets that can be purchased from the Gopher catalog or use the pickle buckets that the cooks have in the school cafeteria. Stacking cups can also be used—the same cups used for cup-stacking activities. The size of the bucket or cup does not matter.

Equipment
- Twelve buckets of any size (preferably buckets that are different colors, such as 3 yellow, 3 red, 3 blue, and 3 green buckets)
- Construction key, or a design of the buckets stacked in a certain way (this key can be drawn and provided by the teacher)
- One folding mat

Setup
The area designated by the teacher to build the bucket design is called the construction area. This area should measure about 50 feet (15 meters) by 15 feet (4.5 meters). Within the construction area and at one end of the space, designate where the buckets will be stacked into the design. At the other end of the construction area, place the 12 buckets in random fashion on the floor. Place the mat outside of the construction area about 20 feet (6 meters) away and alongside the construction area.

The team designates the six construction builders. The builders gather in the construction area by the buckets.

The remaining team members are the architects, and they have the construction key and go into the construction office (mat). When the team has decided who the builders and architects are and everyone is in the proper place, the task can begin.

Rules and Sacrifices
1. The architects may not touch the buckets or any builder.
2. Only one bucket can be moved and stacked at a time.
3. Two builders must work together to move each bucket.
4. When moving a bucket to the building site, architects must call the builders by their first name. If last names are used, the bucket must be returned, and two new builders must step forward.
5. The method of moving a bucket by the builders can only be used twice. If two builders use hands, then only one more bucket can be moved by four hands. Hands can be used again but only in combination with another body part of another builder—for example, one builder uses both hands and the other builder uses both arms.

6. If the stacked buckets ever come apart or fall during the building process or if a bucket falls to the floor during the transfer to the building area, the whole task must start again.

7. Construction managers may not use the terms *top*, *front*, or *behind* or call out any color.

8. If any rules are broken, the bucket design must be taken down and returned to the starting area; the building process will start again.

Possible Solutions

The builders must listen closely to the architects and then decide with whom and with what method they are going to transfer the bucket to the building site. The architects must come up with different terms to inform the builders how to place the buckets.

Conclusion of the Task

When the buckets are stacked in the building area and placed in the proper order according to the construction key, the task is complete.

Additions and Variations

- Set a time limit for completion.
- Increase the distance that the buckets must be transferred.
- Put history words or numbers on the buckets. The builders must give the correct spelling of the word or the correct answer to the math problem before the buckets can be moved. The instructor can infuse some classroom academics into this challenge.

Safety Considerations

Caution the builders to work together and move carefully when transferring a bucket.

BUILDING CHARACTER

The team must move a marble from point A to point B. The team must use the seven special marble transports to move the marble. Each transport is named after a character trait:

- Loyalty
- Honesty
- Respect
- Sportsmanship
- Caring
- Pride
- Determination

Equipment

- Seven 14-inch (35-centimeter) PVC marble transport tubes made from 1-1/2-inch-diameter (4-centimeter-diameter) PVC pipe; bevel each end of the tubes and mark each tube with one of the character traits
- One small marble that can easily pass through the PVC transport tubes
- One tennis ball can marked with the word *character*
- Two bases (poly spots), one for the starting point and one for the finish line
- One PVC end cap

Setup

Place the starting base on an end line of a basketball court. Place the marble inside the PVC end cap and put the end cap on the starting base. The seven transport tubes are scattered on the floor around the starting base. Put the finish line base about 30 feet (9 meters) away from the starting base and put the tennis ball can marked *character* on this base. The team gathers around the starting base, and each team member selects a marble transport tube. If there are more team members than transport tubes, the instructor could have more tubes available, one for each team member, or let the team members figure out how everyone should be involved if they do not have a tube for everyone. If more tubes are provided, remember to mark each one with a character trait term.

Rules and Sacrifices

1. The marble may not move toward the character can on base 2 unless it is in a character trait tube.
2. The marble and the character trait tubes may never touch the ground. In addition, the marble may never touch a team member's hands. If the marble falls on the floor, someone may pick it up and take it back to the starting base.

3. No team member may touch more than one character trait tube at a time.

4. If a marble is inside a character trait tube, the person holding that tube may not move his or her feet. If the marble is not inside a tube, the person holding that tube can move anywhere in the work area.

5. Team members may not touch the character can on the finish line base with their hands.

6. If, when attempting to place the marble into the character can on the finish line base, the can tips over and the marble rolls out, the team must start over.

7. Group members cannot use last names or put-downs.

8. If any rule is broken, the team must replace the marble inside the PVC end cap and put the end cap back on the starting base.

Possible Solutions

One team member picks up the PVC end cap and places the marble inside one marble transport tube. The team connects all the tubes as best as they can so the marble can roll through the tubes on its way to the character can. When the marble passes through a tube, the person holding that tube runs to the last tube in line and reconnects with it to keep the marble rolling. When the marble reaches the character can, the team has to determine how to get the marble into the can without dropping it on the floor. One solution may be to lower the tubes to the height of the can and then let the marble roll from the last tube into the can. Another solution is to catch the marble from the last tube into the PVC end cap and then dump the marble into the can.

Conclusion of the Task

The task is complete when the marble is transported from the starting base to the finish line base inside the transport tubes without touching the floor or any team member and is finally resting inside the character can.

Ask the team the following questions:

- How does each character trait tube help to complete each person's character?
- What happens if someone's character is missing one of the character traits?

Additions and Variations

- Make the distance between the starting base and finish line base greater or smaller depending on the age of the students.
- Place obstacles between the start and finish base, forcing the team to go around, under, or over the obstacles.
- Time the transport and attempt to set a transport record.

Safety Considerations

Students should be careful not trip over one another while transporting a marble by being aware of the proximity of their teammates.

References

Katz, L. 1993. "All About Me." *American Educator* 17: 18-23.

Chapter 7

Intermediate Challenges

Intermediate challenges are a little more difficult than introductory challenges. They usually involve the use of more equipment, and groups need more time and more teamwork to achieve success.

ISLAND ESCAPE

Island Escape is a favorite challenge of many age groups. This task requires a group to transfer its members across a large, open space using a series of islands. Each island has specific equipment that the group may use (options for equipment substitutions are listed below). Students must transfer from island to island without skipping islands. As part of the uniqueness of this challenge, the group must leave the designated equipment at each island when the last person leaves that island. In this environmentally sound challenge, groups may use the resources, but they are not to abuse them.

All group members must transfer across the gym, stopping at each of the designated islands. When the group completes the challenge, the equipment originally assigned to each island must remain there, except one scooter. That scooter may be with the group members as they stand on their side of the lake. Group members may not skip islands, nor may they send teammates so far ahead that islands between team members are empty.

Equipment

- Five hula hoops or tires for the islands
- Six scooters
- Five long jump ropes
- Five balloons or cones, preferably 18-inch (45-centimeter) cones
- A space approximately the length of a standard basketball court and 10 to 15 feet (3.0 to 4.5 meters) wide

Setup

Place the hula hoops (or tires) in a zigzag fashion about 15 feet (4.5 meters) apart. Place one jump rope, one balloon or cone, and one scooter in each hula hoop. Place one scooter at the starting line (the edge of the lake). The hula hoops (islands) should be slightly farther apart then the length of the jump ropes. You can use one more or one fewer island if your work space dictates a change.

Rules and Sacrifices

1. If a group member touches the floor, that person and the person who has advanced the farthest must return to the beginning.
2. If a sacrifice occurs after people are across the lake, the group may take one scooter back to the starting area.
3. The group may not skip an island. If a group member advances so far ahead that an island between that person and a teammate is unoccupied, the person ahead must go back one island before another group member attempts to advance.
4. Group members cannot move the hula hoops (or tires).
5. Group members cannot use last names or put-downs.

In Island Escape, teammates have to think carefully about
how they use resources.

© Gopher Sport

Possible Solutions

The common solution to this task has the group sending one team member to
the first island. The first member uses the scooter provided. The team carefully
pushes the first person to (or at least toward) the first hula hoop (or tire). That
person sends the scooter back to the group members on shore. As the team sends
a second person, the first person uses the jump rope on the island to help pull the
second person to that island.

At this point, the group may begin to do two things at once. One person can
begin moving toward the second island while a teammate sends a scooter back to
the starting line. The group can send a third person toward the first island while
the first two people work on getting one of them to the second island. Group
members do not have to advance in any specific order, but they must not skip
islands or leave unoccupied islands between group members.

An advantage to using cones for this challenge is that team members can use
them to help balance themselves or use them as oars to help propel a scooter to
the next island. We have had students put the cones between their feet and hop
to the next island.

Groups can tie scooters together to make travel easier. Although the procession from one island to the next is somewhat slow, there is a significant amount of group interaction, and group members must provide a great deal of help to one another.

Conclusion of the Task

The group masters the challenge when all group members have traversed all the islands and have safely reached the opposite shore. They must leave one scooter, one balloon or cone, and one jump rope at each island when they leave.

Additions and Variations

- Have groups carry objects across the lake (wounded group members) or add additional obstacles in the lake.
- Eliminate the use of hopping on the cones because this tactic allows group members to work independently without helping one another.
- Tie scooters together for students needing accommodations.

Safety Considerations

Because participants use scooters in this challenge, go over the safety issues related to their use. Remind students to be careful if they push teammates using the scooters. Group members often get off the scooters, climb onto the tires, and then later get back on the scooters. Although participants are only a few inches (centimeters) off the ground, they can fall or slip getting on a scooter if they are not careful. Groups often pass scooters from island to island without anyone on them. Participants must not throw scooters or push them so hard that someone is hit or a scooter interferes with another group.

PLUNGER BALL

Plunger Ball is a unique challenge that requires a group to build a conveyor system to transfer basketballs from a designated area into a basketball hoop. In addition, the balls must drop through the hoop into another container. Group members must devise a plan to move the balls without touching them with their hands. They use certain pieces of equipment to manipulate the basketballs.

Group members must work together to form a conveyor using the five sets of ti-nikling poles. The basketballs must travel down the sets of poles toward the designated basketball hoop. In addition, as the group is transferring the basketballs, the balls must be over the heads of those holding the poles. As a ball comes across the last set of poles, some of the group members must help lift the ball onto the tall plunger. To accomplish this part of the challenge, group members use the small plungers to guide or lift the ball. They then need to lift the ball carefully up to the designated basket, drop it into the hoop, and then catch it in a large container resting on the floor. After group members get a ball into the receiving cart, they repeat the procedure with the next ball.

Equipment

- Five sets of poles 8 to 10 feet (250 to 300 centimeters) long
- Three basketballs
- Three deck tennis rings on which to place the basketballs
- Four small bathroom plungers
- One plunger mounted onto a 5- to 6-foot (150- to 180-centimeter) mop handle
- One large container such as a custodial cart

Setup

You need a space about three-fourths the size of a basketball court (see diagram). Set the three basketballs onto the deck tennis rings. Place the rings on one free throw line (three-quarters of the distance from the basket to which the group will travel). Set the poles in pairs lying end to end down the center of the basketball court. Set two small plungers at each end of the line of poles. Place the tall plunger near the designated hoop into which the basketballs must fall. Set the large container under the basket.

Rules and Sacrifices

1. If a ball touches the floor, the group must start at the beginning.
2. If a ball touches any part of a group member's body, the ball must go back to the starting position. The one exception is that the ball may roll over the hands of those holding the poles.
3. A group member may hold on to only one plunger at a time. If a group member holds on to two or more plungers, the group must return the ball to the beginning position.

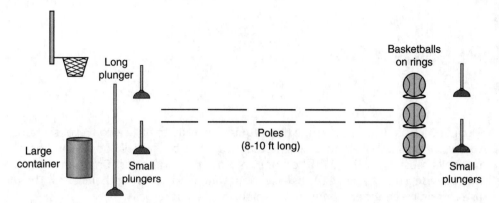

Plunger Ball setup.

4. When the ball goes through the basketball hoop, it must fall into the large container. If it misses, the group must return the ball to the beginning position.

5. Group members cannot use last names or put-downs.

Possible Solutions

The most common solution is to have two group members, each holding a small plunger, lift a basketball onto the first set of poles. Two other group members hold the poles. Those holding the poles may be standing, kneeling, or lying on the floor. These group members try to roll the ball across the set of poles and transfer it to the next set of poles. The two group members with the plungers may help steady or guide the ball as it rolls along the poles. The ball makes its way across all five sets of poles. As the ball reaches the end of the line, one group member holds the tall plunger (a plunger head placed on a mop handle or broom handle, 5 to 6 feet [150 to 180 centimeters] long). Other group members may use the other available plungers to lift or guide the ball onto the tall plunger. The group then slowly lifts the ball toward the basketball hoop. As the ball drops through the hoop, it must land into the large designated receiving container (a large garbage can or custodial cart works well). One or more group members may try to manipulate the cart so that the basketball falls into it.

Groups may choose slightly different ways to hold the poles. Group members might work in pairs so that two people work with a set of two poles. These people may have to set their poles down and go to another set after they transfer the ball to the adjacent set of poles. Some groups may use a method of having some group members at the ends of two different sets of poles to create a railroad track effect.

Groups may stand, kneel, or lie on the floor as long as the ball moves above group members' heads from one set of poles to the next.

Conclusion of the Task

The group completes the task when all the balls go through the basketball hoop and successfully land in the receiving cart or large container.

Additions and Variations

- You may choose the number of balls that you have the groups use. We recommend three basketballs.

Groups may choose different ways to hold the poles.

- The challenge is more difficult if group members are required to stand when transferring the balls from one set of poles to another.
- If you do not have tinikling poles, use plastic PVC plumbing pipe. Pipe that is 1.5 inches (4 centimeters) in diameter is fine. Use 8- to 10-foot (2.5- to 3-meter) lengths. You can find plungers at discount stores, outlet stores, hardware stores, or full-service lumber and remodeling businesses.

You may find additions or variations that meet your needs. Because this challenge is time consuming and requires a lot of group participation and interaction, other variations may not be necessary.

Safety Considerations

Group members need to use caution when manipulating the poles. Someone can easily lose concentration or forget where teammates are positioned. If this happens, a person may drop the poles on a teammate. Rarely would the ball dropping on someone cause injury. Group members must handle the plungers carefully to avoid hitting teammates.

Teammates should be careful with poles and plungers to avoid hitting teammates.

THE MAZE

Two students in a team-building class for Saint Mary's University of Minnesota presented us with The Maze. We consider this challenge one of the standards for any group participating in a team-building program. It's easy to change the level of difficulty and do this activity in a limited space with little equipment. The Maze can be done in a classroom setting as well.

The Maze could also be called the memory game. Most participants are familiar with memory game activities and usually feel comfortable or confident the first time they see this task. Group members need to discover a path through the maze by trial and error. During the challenge, the group receives a signal if a group member makes an error going through the maze. Correct moves are noted by no signal. The group must memorize correct moves so that each person going through the maze can respond to the correct pathway. We recommend using the 16-base maze before trying a maze with more bases.

Equipment

- Sixteen poly spots or vinyl bases (or carpet squares)

Note: If you choose to make a larger maze, add the corresponding bases to your equipment list.

Create the basic maze by using 16 poly spots or vinyl bases.

Setup

Set the bases or spots in four rows of four bases, spaced 12 to 24 inches (30 to 60 centimeters) apart. If you have options for color, we recommend that the starting base be one color and the other bases be a different color. If you are setting up a few different challenges at one time, place this challenge in a small space.

The instructor creates a maze ahead of time (see diagram). The instructor can monitor the challenge or put one group member in charge of beeping his or her teammates off the path when an error occurs. We recommend an oral "beep" or "buzz" to designate an incorrect move. We also suggest that the group be told where the entry spot is located. The group must then discover the path and the exit base.

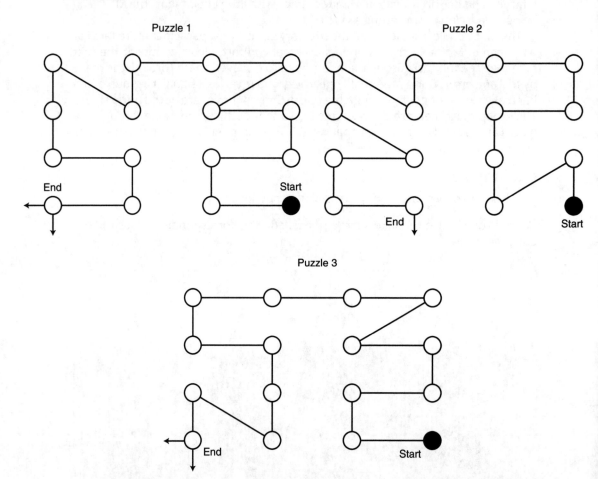

Puzzle 1

Puzzle 2

Puzzle 3

Teachers can make up their own mazes once these examples become familiar to students.

Rules and Sacrifices

1. If a group member steps on a wrong base, his or her turn ends, and the next person begins.
2. Once a person steps off a base or spot, it is considered a move.
3. A person may not step back to a previous base.

4. When attempting the second maze, no one may speak or use any type of oral communication. If this happens, the person moving through the maze must step out of the maze and let the next person begin.

5. Group members cannot use last names or put-downs. If this happens, the person traveling through the maze must step off the path and let the next person begin.

Possible Solutions

The solutions follow the designated paths created ahead of time (see diagram). Groups will need varying amounts of time to solve the problem. Groups discover solutions only through trial and error.

Conclusion of the Task

A group completes the challenge when every group member successfully follows the correct path through the maze. As an example, if Audrey makes it through the maze, she is done. If Jordan follows and makes an error, he must wait until the other group members try to make it through the maze before he takes another turn. Once through, group members may help their teammates figure out the correct path. For the group to be successful, everyone must make it through the maze.

Additions and Variations

- To increase the difficulty, add rows of bases. Instead of four rows of four, use five rows of five.

- Reduce the forms of communication that team members can use. An example of would be disallowing any oral forms of communication, prohibiting any type of hand or foot signals, or not allowing group members to touch one another physically while moving through the maze.

- Give each group two different mazes to conquer. The second maze should have at least one variation or change. For example, students may not use verbal communication.

Safety Considerations

Unless you choose a variation of this challenge that requires participants to be blindfolded, no perceived safety considerations apply to this challenge. If you use blindfolds, refer to the Blindfolds section in chapter 4 about how to use them.

STEPPING STONES I

Stepping Stones I can be a difficult challenge to master, but groups can solve it using many different solutions. The difficulty of the task lies in the reluctance of most students to touch someone physically. Verbal communication is exceptionally important in solving this challenge.

In this task, students stand in a specific order, using bases placed in a straight line, and then reverse their order by moving from base to base.

Lay out a straight line of bases on the floor, 12 to 15 inches (30 to 38 centimeters) apart. The students begin on a base and then move from base to base until they are in reverse order from their starting positions. Use one more base than you have group members (for example, with eight students, use nine bases) so that students can shift positions. Group members need to help one another move and maintain their balance, which is vital to this task.

Equipment

- One base for each group member
- One extra base
- Extra bases for large groups

Note: Flat, indoor bases are best. If you have no bases, tape 12- to 15-inch (30- to 38-centimeter) squares on the floor or use carpet squares cut to that size.

Setup

Outline the bases with tape so that students know where the bases belong and the bases remain stationary. This procedure also helps you set up the task for the next class or the next day.

You may want to have students take a number (1 through 8) to help them remember their positions at the end of the challenge.

Rules and Sacrifices

This task has many rules, so the group needs extra time for reading.

1. Only one person may touch a base at a time.
2. When moving from base to base, a person may move in either direction to a neighboring base.
3. Group members may touch a new base only if it is empty.
4. Group members cannot move the bases except to make minor adjustments; no penalty is necessary if the group member does not get off the base to adjust it.
5. Shoes are considered part of the person, which means that participants may not remove their shoes, put them on the floor, and use them as extra stepping stones.

6. No one may touch the floor with any part of the body.

7. If a group member breaks any rule, the entire group must start the task again.

The rule prohibiting more than one group member from touching the same base at the same time does not mean that a group member cannot lift or hold a teammate off an occupied base or step on the feet of a teammate to move along.

Possible Solutions

In the most common solution to this challenge, a person on one end works toward the other end by jumping or stepping over neighbors, who squat as low as possible. The student on the move, of course, needs an empty base on which to step. Consider the following example: The group needs to leave an empty base between Ann and Ericka so that a base is available for Seth. Ann gets as low as possible so that Seth can step or leap over her. Ericka prepares to help Seth keep his balance. (Another approach is for Ann and Seth to exchange positions.) After Seth goes by, Ann moves to the end base, where Seth began. Seth moves over next to Ann, and Ericka moves next to Seth, leaving an empty base between Ericka and Matt. Seth tries to get past Ericka to the next position, and Matt prepares to assist Seth. The group continues this procedure until Seth makes it to the opposite end of the line. Then it's Ann's turn. She moves down the line until she is next to Seth. Then it's Ericka's turn, then Matt's, then Megan's, and so on until the group has fully reversed its order.

Rather than jump or step over each other, teammates could step on their neighbor's shoes (without touching the base) and move to the next base. Group members could lift one another over to a new base. Leapfrogging over one another is another option.

Regardless of the method used, teammates need to help each other maintain their balance so that no one touches the floor or touches a base already occupied. The size of the bases allows little margin of error for maintaining balance. Group members who work well together will have nonmoving members reaching toward their teammates to support them physically.

In the most common solution to this challenge, a person on one end works toward the other end by jumping or stepping over neighbors, who squat as low as possible.

A difficulty observed in this challenge is that when a group member makes an error, the group abandons its first plan and attempts a different solution. Another problem arises when a group attempts an improbable method (such as having group members crawl over the backs of squatting teammates) but does not quickly see the futility of its efforts.

Conclusion of the Task

The group solves the task when its members are standing on the bases in reverse order of their starting positions (cheering joyfully, of course).

Additions and Variations

The section on possible solutions covered some variations. Groups whose members do not work well together find this a difficult challenge, but groups whose members are willing to help each other can do this task quickly.

Safety Considerations

Tape the bases to the floor so that they do not move or slide when group members move from base to base (see Poly Spots and Vinyl Bases section in chapter 4). Tell participants that if a solution causes pain, it probably is not a good solution. We have listened to groups discuss the solution of having members crawl over the backs of teammates who place themselves in squatting positions. Occasionally, group members lose their balance and fall to the floor. Remind participants that they must always be prepared to help their teammates. We often see participants watch their teammates lose their balance and fall to the floor but forget to reach out to help them.

Bridge Over the Raging River

Bridge Over the Raging River is a terrific challenge that requires all group members to be integral parts of the solution as they cross a river using four automobile tires, two 8-foot-long (2.5-meter-long) boards, and two ropes. This challenge is not intellectually difficult, but most groups find it physically difficult.

Group members travel from one end of a space (land) to the other end without touching the floor (river). The length of a basketball court works well. The group must carry all equipment to the other side.

Equipment

- Four automobile tires (large tires are harder to use)
- Two 8-foot (2.5-meter) two-by-fours (boards about 3.8 centimeters thick and 9.0 centimeters wide)
- Two jump ropes as shown in the diagram (8- to 14-foot [2.5- to 4.0-meter] lengths of sash cord work best)

Setup

Label distinct starting and ending lines and use a straight-line open area (the length of a gymnasium) free from any objects or walls.

The group creates a series of movable bridges using the two-by-fours to close the gaps between tires. Groups often use one tire as an island to stand on as group members transfer equipment forward. They tie the jump ropes to a tire or two-by-four to pull the equipment forward.

Remind participants that they must move the two-by-fours safely. They must be careful not to hit teammates accidentally with a board or step on one end of a board so that it flips up.

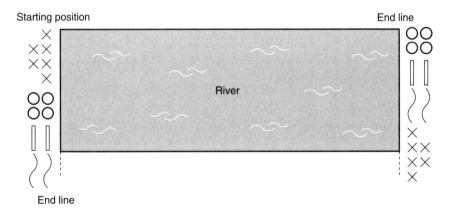

Starting and ending positions for Bridge Over the Raging River.

Rules and Sacrifices

1. Group members may not touch the river (floor).
2. A group member may not step on a two-by-four if it has one end in the river (the two-by-four may sag into and touch the river without penalty).
3. If a group member breaks a rule, the group must take the bridge back to the starting position and start over.
4. Group members cannot use last names or put-downs.

All group members are integral parts of the solution.

Possible Solutions

Most groups follow one basic pattern to solve this task. Groups make a movable bridge. As the group advances, it passes the tires and two-by-fours forward. Group members must share space on a tire.

Participants need good balance and must hold on to or physically assist teammates throughout the challenge. They have no choice but to help one another constantly! The group also needs to communicate how it intends to pass the equipment along. If someone tries to roll a tire to a teammate who is unaware of the plan, the tire may roll off course, causing an unwanted detour. Participants may attempt to move tires by getting their feet inside a tire and jumping along with it (hard to do but possible). Most groups attempting the challenge find it difficult to have several teammates balance on a tire at once. Multiple mistakes often occur, which generally means that the group must start the task over.

Conclusion of the Task

The group is successful when it crosses the river (the length of the gymnasium or basketball court) with all assigned equipment in its possession. You may institute a time limit, basing success on criteria other than crossing the river. When group members complete the challenge, have them take the equipment back to the starting position for the next group to use.

Additions and Variations

- Smaller tires, such as boat trailer tires of 11 to 12 inches (28 to 30 centimeters), create a crowded area and make it more difficult for several people to maintain good balance.
- You might place obstacles (cones, balance beams, parallel bars) in the river that the group must travel around, over, or under.
- Another variation is to have the group carry some object, such as a football blocking dummy, that represents an injured group member who must be rescued.

Safety Considerations

Participants need to move the two-by-fours carefully. They must not drop them, leave them standing on end, throw them, jerk them, or otherwise handle them recklessly. We have already mentioned that participants must avoid stepping on one end of a board if the other end is not supported. If a board were to flip up, it could hit someone, an especially painful event if a teammate is straddling the board with his or her feet. Teammates should not grab one another and cause one or both to fall off the bridge in a careless manner. This challenge includes a lot of lifting and moving of tires. Participants need to lift properly and safely.

JUMPING MACHINE

Jumping Machine challenges a group to complete 10 consecutive jumps over a turning long rope.

The group selects two members to turn the long rope as they would a jump rope. Other group members try to jump the rope 10 consecutive times. The entire group (minus the turners) must jump the rope at the same time. The rope turners may change places with a jumper who needs to rest.

Equipment

- One long rope
- A space large enough to turn the rope safely as a jump rope

Note: Because the rope is long, you may need the space of up to half a basketball court. If you do not have a long enough rope, tie two long jump ropes together. (Ropes made of sash cord are better than speed ropes.) If you have enough rope, you might try tying ropes parallel to one another to make a strand two or three ropes thick and 25 to 30 feet (7.5 to 9.0 meters) long.

Setup

Many groups assume that this is an easy challenge—and for some it may be—but to be successful, the group needs a plan for entering the turning rope and may need to have several group members practice turning the long rope. The jumpers can't jump well if the rope turners don't turn the rope well. Because of the weight

All group members (except the turners) must jump at the same time.

and length of the rope, it must travel through a high arc. To accomplish this, the rope turners need to use their upper body strength. The rope turners need not hold the long rope at the ends, so they should try different ways of turning the rope to find the best hand placement. The weight of the rope, rather than the length, is what adds difficulty to this challenge.

Rules and Sacrifices

1. Only one group member may be at each end of the rope. All other group members are jumpers.
2. To be counted, the jumps must be consecutive.
3. The rope must pass over the jumpers' heads and below their feet.
4. If they miss, the jumpers begin the task again.
5. The turners do not have to hold the very end of the long rope.
6. Group members cannot use last names or put-downs.

Possible Solutions

We generally find that a group will use either of two approaches to this challenge. One solution has the jumpers standing in a straight line, close together, 1 to 2 feet (30 to 60 centimeters) apart. On a signal, all jumpers start jumping at the same time. In the second solution, the jumpers start jumping the rope one or two at a time; the group does not start counting jumps until all team members have entered the turning rope.

If the rope turners get tired or have trouble doing their job, teammates could take their place. If new turners take over, they should have a chance to practice.

Rarely will a group be immediately successful with this challenge. Because of repeated failures, groups often try to circumvent the rules, often by slowing the speed of the turning rope so that group members can step over the rope in slow motion. The group must turn the rope at a challenging pace.

Conclusion of the Task

The group masters the challenge by completing 10 consecutive jumps. Group members should count their successful jumps aloud so that they always know the status of their effort. When the group counts aloud, the teacher won't have to watch the group all the time because the nature of the counting usually causes students to be dependable and honest.

Additions and Variations

Challenge the group to devise a plan to exit the turning rope successfully.

Safety Considerations

Jumpers should not fall deliberately or act silly while jumping. We have gone away from using a tug-of-war rope in this activity. Some tug-of-war ropes are extremely heavy and could hurt a jumper, especially if the rope hits the jumper in the head. A heavy rope could also knock the feet out from under a jumper, causing a fall.

HUMAN PEGS

Human Pegs is a challenge that resulted from a class assignment in one of our summer classes. Bill Butterman and Ryan Johnson helped create this challenge along with Dan Midura. This challenge is an adaptation of a children's game that uses golf tees or marbles that are placed on a wooden board. The object of the game is to jump the pegs, remove the jumped pegs from the game, and wind up with only one peg. In this adaptation, the pegs are group members who try to jump each other, one at a time, until only one person remains on the playing area.

Create a triangular play area with 10 bases, equally spaced from one another (see diagram). Each group member stands on one base. If you do not have nine team members in the group, you can place a tall cone on a base in place of a person.

Human Pegs setup.

Equipment

- Ten vinyl bases, poly spots, or carpet squares to create the game board
- Tall cones to serve as substitutes for real bodies if a group does not have nine members
- An area about 8 feet (2.5 meters) square

Setup

Set the bases an equal distance from one another, approximately 12 inches (30 centimeters) apart. The setup forms a triangle. Group members can choose where each person stands, and they place cones on bases where needed. If a group leaves bases 5, 1, 7, or 10 open, they will be unable to reach a solution. We suggest that you let group members struggle to discover these things themselves.

Rules and Sacrifices

1. Group members may not touch the floor before they are eliminated.
2. Team members may go over one another to a new base. They may not walk around one another.
3. Only one person may touch a base at a time.
4. Group members can make moves only by jumping over one base at a time. Teammates may not simply step from one base to an open base.
5. Group members cannot use last names or put-downs.
6. If a group member breaks a rule, all group members get back on a base, but they must leave a new base open as the empty base.

Possible Solutions

We have provided six different solutions. With 10 bases and team members occupying 9 of them, a group cannot do the task if it leaves base 5 open. A group will be unable to get down to one person remaining if it leaves bases 1, 7, or 10 open to start the activity. Groups must leave bases 2, 3, 4, 6, 8, or 9 as the open base (see table 7.1).

Conclusion of the Task

The group should be able to complete the task within a few attempts. If the challenge seems too easy, have group members show you the solution after they have completed the challenge. Require them to prove their solution to you. Their turn ends when no member can make a jump. If they do not get down to one player, have them try again.

Additions and Variations

- This task can be done by adding another row of 5 bases to make a pattern of 15 bases, meaning that people or cones must occupy 14 bases.
- To simplify the challenge, allow group members simply to walk around to another base as their move rather than jump a teammate.
- To make the challenge more difficult, space the bases farther apart.
- Eliminate oral communication during the challenge.
- To modify this activity for a team as small as one or two, use cones and don't have any people on the bases.

Safety Considerations

This challenge does not present obvious safety considerations. If jumping over teammates becomes a requirement for this challenge, make certain that the bases or poly spots do not slide on the floor.

Table 7.1 Human Pegs Possible Solutions

Open space 2	Open space 3	Open space 4	Open space 6	Open space 8	Open space 9
7 to 2	10 to 3	1 to 4	1 to 6	10 to 8	7 to 9
9 to 7	8 to 10	7 to 2	10 to 3	3 to 10	10 to 8
1 to 4	1 to 6	9 to 7	8 to 10	7 to 9	3 to 10
6 to 1	4 to 1	2 to 9	3 to 8	2 to 7	8 to 3
7 to 2	10 to 3	10 to 8	7 to 9	10 to 8	1 to 6
1 to 4	1 to 6	3 to 10	2 to 7	7 to 9	4 to 1
4 to 6	6 to 4	7 to 9	10 to 8	9 to 2	10 to 3
10 to 3	7 to 2	10 to 8	7 to 9	1 to 4	1 to 6
End on 3	End on 2	End on 8	End on 9	End on 4	End on 6

Teamwork Walk

The Teamwork Walk challenge is easy to understand but hard to do. Groups enjoy solving it, but it requires practice and teamwork. Every group member plays an equal role in solving the task.

The group tries to follow a designated path, usually the length or perimeter of a basketball court. The group uses team skis, made of long two-by-six boards (boards about 3.8 centimeters thick and 14.0 centimeters wide) or four-by-four beams (about 9.0 centimeters square) with rope-type handles so that group members can hold on to the skis while trying to move the skis. You may need to construct the team skis because it is hard to find commercially made skis that allow more than six people to participate at one time.

Equipment
- Team skis or long walking boards made of two 12-foot (3.6-meter) two-by-six or four-by-four pine or fir boards (length can vary to meet your needs)
- Sash cord, clothesline rope, or strapping material to make the handholds

This challenge is easy to understand but hard to do.

Drill holes through the two-by-sixes so that the rope or strapping material can pass through the boards. If you drill the holes about 18 inches (45 centimeters) apart, you can fit eight or nine sets of handholds on a 12-foot (3.6-meter) board. Group members should be able to remove their feet from the skis easily if they fall.

Setup

Provide the group with a set of team skis and a designated walking path. The path should be long enough to make the challenge interesting. Remember that the skis are 8 to 12 feet (2.5 to 3.5 meters) long, so choose a space that allows a sufficient challenge and adequate turning space.

Rules and Sacrifices

1. Group members may not touch the floor with any part of their bodies.
2. Group members may not use walls or stationary structures to help them maintain their balance.
3. If a group member breaks a rule, the group starts over.
4. Group members cannot use last names or put-downs.

Possible Solutions

Teamwork is the solution for this challenge. Using a group leader or organizer helps because someone must coordinate the team's movements. For instance, team members must move their feet simultaneously. Having someone count the cadence helps. Group members may need to assist one another physically by holding on to the hips, waist, or shoulders of the group member directly in front of them. When turning, clear verbal communication is essential. Be aware that if one person falls during the task, others may, too. Deliberate carelessness could put teammates into precarious positions.

Conclusion of the Task

The group is successful when it crosses the finish line. (Decide whether a team finishes when the first person reaches the finish line or when the entire team crosses the finish line.)

Additions and Variations

- Groups must complete the challenge within a time limit.
- Use both a time limit and distance goal. How far can the group travel in a given time? A large gymnasium or long hall lends itself well to this variation.
- Devise an obstacle course or zigzag path or require specific turns as variations. A 360-degree turn might be a tough challenge.
- Don't let students hold on to one another.
- Place a number of objects along the path for the group to pick up, such as a ball, jump rope, base, or hoop. The team stops to let team members pick up one object each.
- Send the group under a lowered parallel bar or volleyball net. This challenge generates a lot of laughter and fun.

Safety Considerations

Because participants are working in a line, one person ahead of another, the group must avoid falling like dominoes if someone should lose his or her balance. Many commercially made buddy boards or team walkers allow only two, four, or six teammates to work at one time, but they do incorporate handheld ropes. We, too, have moved away from footholds to handheld ropes, which allow participants to remove themselves from the skis more quickly if the group loses its balance.

STOMP IT

In this challenge, one group member stomps on the ball launcher while the rest of the group members attempt to catch the balls hurled into the air before they touch the ground.

The team must decide which group member will stomp on the ball launcher to launch the balls. The remaining group members must stand or kneel on poly spots or bases surrounding the launcher and catch the flung balls before they touch the ground. If any launch attempt fails, the group rotates so that a new group member becomes the launcher.

Equipment

- A ball launcher or stomp-it board with five or six holes and five or six different colored balls
- Poly spots or bases on which to stand or kneel

Note: If you cannot find a commercial six-hole stomp-it board, it is easy to make. Using a flat board approximately 2.5 feet (76 centimeters) wide by 12 to 18 inches (30 to 45 centimeters) wide, drill 6 holes on one end, large enough to support a ball. Put a fulcrum underneath the board, approximately 6 inches (5 centimeters) from the end on the opposite side of where the balls are located.

Setup

Place the stomp-it board on the floor or on a firm tumbling mat. Place the balls in the launcher holes. Set poly spots or bases around the ball launcher a few feet (a meter or so) from the launching device.

Group members must stand or kneel on the poly spots or bases until the stomper hits the launcher with his or her foot.

Rules and Sacrifices

1. If teammates do not catch all the balls, the balls are replaced on the ball launcher, and the group rotates so that a new group member becomes the stomper.
2. Group members must catch all the balls in one stomp attempt.
3. A group member may catch only one ball.
4. Anytime a ball touches the floor, a new stomper rotates to the ball launcher and takes a turn stomping.
5. Group members cannot use last names or put-downs.

Possible Solutions

Group members should study the flight pattern of the balls and communicate that pattern to other members of the team. In addition, the stompers should try to stomp with similar force each time, ensuring that the flight path of the balls is consistent.

Group members should study the flight pattern of the balls.

Conclusion of the Task

The groups having success are usually quite vocal when group members all catch the correct colored balls. Most groups engage in a lot of discussion about stomping force, direction of flight, and who needs to stand where to catch the flying balls. When all five balls are caught at one time—one ball by each team member (not counting the stomper)—the task is complete.

Additions and Variations

- Use a math variation in which each ball has a point value. Team members continue to catch the stomped balls until they reach a point requirement.
- A batter can hit a stomped ball (the stomper launches one ball at a time) and the other team members then catch the batted ball. The team must make a specific number of catches (such as 6 to 10).
- Each group member must catch an assigned ball.
- To make the challenge easier, assign a permanent stomper.

Safety Considerations

Teammates could possibly collide when attempting to catch balls if one teammate's ball crosses paths with another's ball.

GREAT BALLS OF COLOR

This challenge was presented to us in one of our summer graduate classes. Currently, Gopher Sport markets a similar challenge called Cooperative Maze Game. Great Balls of Color uses a homemade sheet with cutout holes, and Cooperative Maze Game uses a manufactured tarp with holes cut out for balls to drop through.

The colored balls must pass through the corresponding colored holes in the sheet into a container beneath the sheet, without touching the floor or any body parts of group members trying to solve the task. Group members hold either the edges of the sheet or a scoop. They manipulate the colored balls by moving the sheet so that the balls fall through the correct holes and land in the catching container. The scoopers attempt to catch any balls that fall off the sheet or fall through the holes in the sheet and do not land in the catching container. Balls that fall off the sheet, pass through the wrong hole, or miss the container must be placed back onto the sheet.

Equipment

- A sheet (twin-size top sheet) with five holes cut out and marked with different colors
- Five colored softball-sized Whiffle balls, with colors corresponding to the holes in the sheet

The group tries to get colored balls to pass through corresponding colored holes in the sheet into a container beneath the sheet.

- A container to catch the balls such as a 5-gallon (20-liter) bucket, a recycling container, or an 18- to 20-gallon-sized (68- to 75-liter-sized) plastic storage bin
- Two scoops (manufactured scoops or milk jugs with the ends cut out)

The Cooperative Maze Game set, from Gopher Sport, has all the equipment except the scoops and container.

Setup

You need an area only slightly larger than the size of the sheet. A space the size of a basketball free throw lane will work. Team members may hold the corners and sides of the sheet or tarp. Place the container under the middle of the sheet. Scoopers may move around and under the sheet. Group members then place the balls on the sheet.

Rules and Sacrifices

1. The hands of group members must remain on the edges of the sheet or tarp.
2. No hands or other body part may touch a ball.
3. Group members may not move the container.
4. If a ball goes through the wrong hole, the group must start the task again (unless a scooper catches the ball).
5. If a ball touches the ground, the group must start the task again.
6. Scoopers may catch a ball that falls off the sheet or through the wrong hole. If they make the catch, they place the ball back on the sheet.
7. Scoopers may not touch the sheet with their bodies or the scoop.
8. Group members cannot use last names or put-downs.

Possible Solutions

This challenge has one basic solution. Group members lift and lower the sheet to maneuver the balls from side to side. They must direct the balls through the correct holes and have them land in the container. Teammates holding the sheet often want to use their feet to kick the ball from beneath the sheet. This tactic breaks rule 2. To achieve success, group members should remain calm. Frequently, a group member makes a rapid movement or jerks the sheet to redirect the path of a ball. This action often causes the ball to fly up or off the sheet.

If you buy the Cooperative Maze Game, be aware that the rules sent with the challenge differ from those presented here. You can do the challenge with either method. The balls with the manufactured challenge are foam and therefore a little lighter.

Conclusion of the Task

A group completes the challenge when all the colored balls pass through the corresponding holes in the sheet and land in the container beneath the sheet.

Additions and Variations

- Do not allow talking.
- Designate one communicator to speak.
- Allow the scoopers to direct the ball into the container from beneath the sheet.

- Allow group members holding the sheet to block the ball with their bodies to keep it from falling off the sheet.
- Allow balls that have passed through the correct holes and fallen in the container to remain there if another ball touches the floor or a group member.
- Try one ball at a time for younger children.

In the initial version of this challenge, the middle hole in the sheet was colored black. No ball could pass through that hole. Only four other colored balls were used. These balls passed through the holes closest to the corners. If a ball passed through the black hole, the group started the challenge from the beginning.

Safety Considerations

This challenge does not present obvious safety considerations. If group members do not know the location of the container, however, they could trip over it if the group holding the sheet moves significantly from its starting position.

Juggler's Carry

This challenge, created as a project in one of our classes by Jeff Lagoo, Kim Poppin, and Tammy Bernard, has some similarities to The Whole World in Their Hands. The challenge uses four large balls.

The team must transfer four large balls halfway across a gym space (such as a basketball court). The group makes four trips; on each trip, the group adds one ball. On the first trip, the group transports one ball. On the second trip, the group adds another ball and transports two. This process continues until the team completes the fourth trip by transporting four balls.

Equipment
- Four large inflatable or rubber balls
- A rope 20 to 30 feet (6 to 9 meters) long
- Two chairs or large cones to create a barrier

Note: We suggest using either a 48-inch (120-centimeter) ball and three smaller balls, a 32-inch (80-centimeter) ball, a 24-inch (61-centimeter) ball, and a 22-inch (56-centimeter) ball, or four 32- to 36-inch (80- to 92-centimeter) balls. The balls could be the light rubber roto-molded balls, beach balls, or cage balls. They can be inflatable or another type of ball approximately these sizes. The size of the balls depends largely on the age and size of your students. As an example, four 22-inch (56-centimeter) balls work with primary-aged children.

Setup
Place two balls behind the start–finish line, which could be the end line of the basketball court. Place two more balls in the center of the gym behind the half court line. If no basketball court is available, mark two lines with tape 30 to 50 feet (9 to 15 meters) apart. In the middle of the area, place two chairs with a rope tied between them. The rope should be about the height of the participants' knees.

Rules and Sacrifices
1. No ball may touch the floor between the starting and finish lines.
2. Team members may not touch the balls with their hands.
3. A different person or different group of people must pick up a ball on each trip.
4. When traveling across the gym, all team members must be connected to one another and must be touching a ball.
5. Group members cannot use last names or put-downs.
6. If a team member breaks a rule, the team must start over from the line where it completed the last successful trip.

Possible Solutions
Students need to communicate about who is picking up the ball and how they will transport it with everyone touching the ball. During each trip, students add a

Team members must avoid using their hands to transport the balls.

ball to the group support system and move with the whole group supporting the balls. Alternatively, team members may decide to break into smaller groups but still maintain a connection to one another as they transport the balls.

Conclusion of the Task

The group completes the task when all four balls pass across the original starting line, now serving as the finish line.

Additions and Variations

- If the team touches the rope, it must restart the task from the previous ball.
- Require the team to find a different way to pick up the ball and add it to the group trip.
- Make the trips longer or shorter.
- Depending on the age of the team, use two or three smaller balls.

Safety Considerations

This challenge presents a few safety considerations. If participants walk backward, teammates should coach them to prevent anyone from tripping. Stepping over the rope obstacle should also elicit help from teammates if the obstacle is hard to see because of the method that the group uses to move the balls. The rope should be strung in a manner that would cause the rope to fall if touched rather than trip a participant.

FRANKENSTEIN

This beat-the-clock challenge reinforces the structure of the human anatomy. It uses the same skeleton equipment as General Hospital, Emergency Room does. We do not normally make the challenges competitive in nature, but part of the fun of this challenge is trying to do it as fast as possible.

Participants attempt to put together the skeleton puzzle in the shortest time possible. The team has to earn the right to put parts of Frankenstein together by successfully tossing and catching a deck tennis ring. Each time team members have successfully passed the ring, the team gets to add three more bones to Frankenstein. A minimum of seven trips of tossing the ring will be required to build Frankenstein. The group creates a system of tossing, catching, running, and building the puzzle.

Equipment

- One skeleton puzzle
- One deck tennis ring
- One storage crate or container
- Five indoor bases

Setup

Place the bases 10 to 15 feet (3.0 to 4.5 meters) apart in a straight line. Modify the distance depending on the age and ability of your students.

Five team members each stand on a different base. The remaining team members must be in the building area close to base 1. The storage crate holding the skeleton puzzle should be at the opposite end of the work area, or about 15 feet (4.5 meters) from base 5. See diagram.

Frankenstein setup.

Rules and Sacrifices

1. Team members must toss the deck tennis ring from base 1 to base 2. The person on base 2 must catch the ring and successfully turn and toss it to the person on base 3. This process continues until the ring has traveled all the way to base 5 and back to base 1. If a team member drops the ring, it must be sent back to the team member who last tossed it.

2. Once the ring gets back to base 1, the medic runs to the storage crate at the opposite end of the gym and brings back three bones. The medic cannot leave the building area (the lab) until the ring gets back to base 1.

3. When the medic returns, he or she must give the bones to the doctors, who begin assembling the puzzle. When the doctors receive the bones, all players rotate positions. The medic goes to base 1, the person on base 1 goes to base 2, the person on base 2 goes to base 3, the person on base 3 moves to base 4, and the person on base 4 moves to base 5. The person on base 5 becomes a new doctor, and one of the doctors becomes the new medic. Team members cannot rotate positions until the medic returns to the building area with three bones.

4. The ring must make seven successful round trips to get all the puzzle pieces to the building area. After the last medic has delivered the last three puzzle pieces, team members can hustle to the lab and confer about any changes they need to make to Frankenstein to make him complete. When they think that they have put Frankenstein together correctly, the last medic yells, "Lightning." This is the signal to stop the clock. The instructor then checks the puzzle for accuracy. If the puzzle is correct, the time stands. If it is incorrect, the clock starts again as the team rearranges the bones.

This process continues until the team assembles Frankenstein correctly.

Possible Solutions

The team should communicate before the challenge starts about where teammates should position themselves to start the challenge. Certainly, a team would want the best catchers on the bases, and a teammate who is a good doctor should plan to rotate to the lab when most of the bones are there.

Conclusion of the Task

The group completes the task when the team assembles Frankenstein correctly and the clock stops.

Additions and Variations

- Allow team members to assign permanent roles so that they can match the team members' skills with the challenge.
- Lengthen or shorten the distance of the toss.
- Allow participants to bring back more or fewer bones to shorten or lengthen the time of the challenge.

Safety Considerations

This challenge presents no specific safety considerations other than the possibility that the deck tennis ring may hit someone who is not looking when a teammate tosses it.

DYNAMIC BARRIER

Three St. Mary's University students, Don Percival, Patti Percival, and Jean Skore, inspired this challenge. This challenge does not require a lot of equipment and can be adapted to students of all ages. Dynamic Barrier is one of the two challenges that uses a turning jump rope.

The team must pass through the twirling barrier (rope) from one side to the other without touching the rope. In addition, all equipment must pass through the barrier. Because the twirlers or rope turners must also pass through the barrier, the group must decide when to change twirlers.

Equipment

- One long jump rope
- One large 22- to 34-inch (56- to 86-centimeter) ball
- Three deck tennis rings
- One hula hoop
- One gym scooter

Setup

You need a work area large enough to accommodate a turning jump rope. Make sure that participants have sufficient room to run through the rope or scoot through on a scooter. An area too close to a barrier, such as a wall, may impede a group's chance for success and compromise safety. The twirlers must practice turning the rope because their proficiency will be crucial to the group's success.

Rules and Sacrifices

1. All group members and all equipment must pass through the barrier without touching it.

2. Group members must roll the large ball through the barrier, and a group member must accompany it. In other words, a team member and the ball must pass through the barrier together, but the ball must be rolling.

3. Team members must toss the deck tennis rings through the barrier, and a team member on the opposite side must catch them. If a team member drops a ring, the team must start the challenge over from the beginning.

4. The scooter must carry a team member through. The team must decide who will sit on the scooter and then push that person through the barrier. Caution: Teammates may assist and push the scooter and their teammate through, but they must be aware of their proximity to the walls. As soon as the scooter gets through the barrier, the rider should stop it and not coast into teammates or equipment.

5. Two teammates must pass through at the same time while holding the hula hoop.

6. All remaining students on the team must pass through the barrier together. Although they do not have to be connected, they must pass through at the same time. This will require two students who have made it through the barrier to take over the job of twirling (the twirlers have to go through as well).

7. If any teammate or any equipment touches the barrier, then that person or that piece of equipment and all team members who have already successfully passed through the barrier must go back to the start.

8. Group members cannot use last names or put-downs.

Possible Solutions

The rules indicate how groups must solve this challenge. Groups use one basic solution to this challenge, although the order of travel will differ from group to group. The team must decide which team members will pass through the barrier with equipment and which team members will pass through the barrier with other teammates. The team must also decide who will throw and catch the deck tennis rings, who will start as the twirlers, and who will replace the original twirlers when it is their turn to pass through the barrier.

Additions and Variations

- Don't use equipment, but time the team. See how long it takes a team to pass through the barrier one at a time, including the switching of twirlers. The clock stops only when all team members have passed through.

- Have teams try passing through the barrier and back to the starting point all connected together. The team should select its best twirlers because they do not have to pass through in this variation.

- Add equipment from activities used in other curriculum units, such as basketballs, footballs, volleyballs, tennis equipment, and so on.

- Have teams choose an order of travel based on an unusual criterion. Examples include chronological birth date order; numerical order using only the day of the birthday month (August 1 would start before February 3); alphabetical order based on first names, middle names, mothers' first names, or other scheme; or order by height (tallest or shortest starting first).

- Give the group a maximum number of rope turns to get everyone through the barrier or count the number of turns as a competitive feature between teams.

Safety Considerations

Because this challenge uses a scooter, refer to the Scooters section in chapter 4 on safe use of scooters. Please be aware that if the people pushing the scooter push too low, the rider may fall backward and hit their head. Make the pushers push at the shoulders or midback. Group members should not deliberately slide through the turning rope. Teammates who throw objects through the barrier should be certain that the receivers are looking and ready to catch the thrown items. Do not place group members too close to a wall on the ending side of the barrier.

TOWER OF TIRES

The Tower of Tires challenge is a takeoff on a children's game commonly called the Tower of Hanoi, among other names. This challenge is a math game that requires participants to restack a set of items while observing a few simple rules. The result finds the original stack in a different place, but the original order of the items remains the same. This challenge requires little room or equipment.

The challenge uses five tires, each a different size. The tires are numbered 1 through 5, from smallest to largest. Stack the five tires on one large cone so that the largest tire (tire 5) is on the bottom and the smallest tire (tire 1) is on the top. Place two additional large cones about 3 feet (1 meter) to either side of the cone holding the five tires (see diagram). The group moves the tires one at a time, from cone to cone, until the stack of tires rests on a different cone.

Equipment
- Five different-sized tires
- Three large cones, preferably 36-inch (90-centimeter) cones
- Tape for marking numbers on the tires
- A clipboard with paper and pencil for recording the moves

Setup
Set the five tires on one large cone with the largest on the bottom and the smallest on the top. Set the other two cones in line with the middle cone approximately 3 feet (1 meter) to either side.

Rules and Sacrifices
1. The team can move only one tire at a time.
2. A tire may not be stacked on top of a smaller tire.
3. Two teammates must move each tire, with each person using two hands.
4. Each time the team moves a tire, a different combination of teammates must move it.
5. When team members move a tire, they must move it onto a cone (the cone may be empty or have another tire on it). A move is considered complete when one or both teammates let go of the tire.
6. No tire may touch the floor unless it is on a cone.
7. If a team breaks a rule, team members must restack all tires in the original position.
8. Group members cannot use last names or put-downs.

Possible Solutions
The fewest number of moves required to reach the solution is 31. Teams can complete the challenge using more than the minimum number of moves.

Starting position

Solution in progress

Possible ending position

The progression of Tower of Tires from start to finish and somewhere in between.

An example of how a team might perform the challenge follows. Two team-mates move tire 1 onto the empty cone on the right. Two other teammates move tire 2 onto the empty cone on the left. Another combination of two teammates moves tire 1 over to tire 2, allowing yet another combination of teammates to move tire 3 onto the empty cone. This process continues until the team is able to move the bottom tire (tire 5) to a different cone. The team members then try to reverse the process so that they can move tire 4 onto tire 5 and so on, until they restack all the tires.

We suggest that students write down all their moves. The time will likely come when the team has used every possible combination of team members to make a move. When this occurs, the team may repeat combinations on the list.

Conclusion of the Task

As noted previously, the team completes the task when it has moved the entire stack of tires to a different cone with the tires stacked in their original order. Have the group members move the stack of tires back to the center cone before going on to the next challenge.

Additions and Variations

- Three tires can be moved in seven moves (minimum moves).
- Four tires can be moved in 15 moves (minimum moves).

- Five tires can be moved in 31 moves (minimum moves).
- Six tires can be moved in 63 moves (minimum moves).
- Seven tires can be moved in 127 moves (minimum moves).

Safety Considerations

This challenge does not present any inherent safety considerations. As with any task using tires, make sure that no steel belts are exposed. Group members should lift tires safely so that no back muscle problems occur.

FACTOR IN

This is another challenge created by teachers in the team-building program offered through Saint Mary's University of Minnesota. This challenge was created by Marc Bachman and Jay Ehlers. This challenge is unique in that it incorporates math and puzzle skills into a great team-building challenge.

The team must remain connected and move through a maze of numbered bases. The team members must stand on various bases in the maze, but the bases they are using must have a total number that can be factored by three.

Equipment

- Twelve round bases with numbers written or taped on top

Setup

The bases should be set on the floor in the following pattern:

12	11	10
7	8	9
6	5	4
1	2	3

Rules and Sacrifices

1. Team members must stay connected during travel.
2. Team members may only move one base at a time.
3. Team members may move in a straight or diagonal path.
4. Teammates must remain one base away from the immediate person they are connected to.
5. Only one team member may enter the maze at a time. When a teammate gets to the last row of the maze, that teammate may step out of the maze but must stay connected with the others.
6. After each team member enters or exits the maze, the total-sum number (of the bases team members are standing on) must be a factor of three. Otherwise, the team must start again.
7. Only one person on a base at a time.
8. Group members cannot use last names or put-downs.

Possible Solutions

As each team member enters or exits the maze, the team needs to add up the numbers they are standing on. If the numbers add up to a factor of three, the team can continue.

Conclusion of the Task

When the whole team has successfully moved through the maze and is standing together at the finish, the challenge is complete.

Additions and Variations

- To make the challenge easier, eliminate the row with bases 12, 11, and 10.
- To make the challenge more difficult, randomly place the bases. One factor of three should be in each row.
- Time the challenge.
- Add more rows.

Safety Considerations

This challenge does not present obvious safety considerations.

Team Beanbag Toss

The team must successfully toss three beanbags into a hoop during one of three rounds. There are three hoops and three beanbags. The hoops are placed at graduated distances from the team. The team must get three beanbags into each hoop in one try. In other words, the team can't get two beanbags in in one try, leave those two in the hoop, and try again with the remaining beanbag. All three beanbags must land in the hoop in one try. This challenge forces the team to determine who should toss for each hoop. Obviously, the better tossers should toss for the farthest hoop. There will be misses each round; team members must encourage one another.

Equipment
- Three hoops (for younger children, use larger hoops; to make the challenge more difficult, use smaller hoops)
- Gym floor tape to tape the hoops to the floor
- One poly spot

Setup
Set the poly spot at the designated starting point. Tape the hoops to the floor in a straight line from the poly spot. The first hoop should be closest to the poly spot and the second and third hoop successively farther away. For young children, the distances would be much closer than for high school students. For this example, let's assemble the challenge for seventh graders. The first hoop is taped to the floor 10 feet (3 meters) away from the starting line (poly spot). The second hoop is placed 20 feet (6 meters) away from the starting line, and the third hoop is taped to the floor 30 feet (9 meters) away from the starting line. The team must select three tossers to toss each beanbag into the first hoop. All three must land and stay in the hoop in one try. If two go in and one misses, then all three beanbags must be collected, and the same three tossers must try again. It may take several attempts to get all three beanbags in the hoop in one round; this is when the other teammates must encourage the tossers. After three beanbags have successfully made it into hoop 1, three new tossers must attempt to toss them into hoop 2. When that has been accomplished, new tossers attempt to get the beanbags into hoop 3. If there are not enough teammates to have three new tossers for each hoop, the team will have to decide who gets to toss at two different hoops. Teammates not acting as tossers must retrieve beanbags, hand the beanbags to the tossers, and encourage students who may miss. The instructor may decide to bring the hoops closer if he or she decides a team does not have the athletic ability to accomplish this task.

Rules and Sacrifices
1. The tossers must toss from the poly spot. They may step off the poly spot with one foot while tossing.

2. Three beanbags constitute one round; all three beanbags must land in the designated hoop in one round. During that round, the beanbags must be tossed by three different tossers.

3. Team members must retrieve and bring back errant beanbags but may not touch a beanbag in flight.

4. All team members must have at least one chance to toss the beanbags; the tossers cannot be the same team members each round.

5. The team must decide by consensus who should toss twice if needed.

6. The beanbags must hit the floor inside the hoop first; they cannot slide in. Once inside the hoop, the beanbags must stay inside the hoop.

7. Beanbags cannot be tossed back to teammates at the poly spot; they must be brought back and handed to the tossers.

8. Group members cannot use last names or put-downs.

9. If two beanbags are successful and one is not, the team must only start again for that hoop; they do not have to reattempt a hoop that has already been conquered.

Possible Solutions

This will be a very frustrating challenge for a team. A team may not actually solve this challenge; during repeated failures, frustration may mount. It is important that the team stays positive and encourages one another. The only solution is to keep trying and learn from past misses. If a team cannot solve this challenge, it may elect to stop and move to another challenge with the instructor's permission. The instructor can change the distance of the hoops if it proves too difficult for the teams.

Conclusion of Task

When the team has tossed three beanbags into each hoop in one round, the task is complete.

Additions and Variations

- Vary the distance of the hoops.
- Set a time limit, or create a competition and see which team accomplishes this task first.
- Allow the beanbags to slide into the hoop.

Safety Considerations

Do not allow anyone to toss while a retriever is by the designated hoop. Everyone should be behind the tossers while tossing.

I SEE ME

This activity is designed to allow students to explore their own connection to nature and be creative and self-reflective.

Give teams 20 to 30 minutes to simply wander outside and find something of visual interest. This does not have to occur in a special location. Encourage them to pay attention to the small details of nature that they often fail to notice. Once they have identified something of interest, they should take a photo. Cameras will not be provided; team members may use cell phone cameras (noted in the Equipment section). Each team member should take three photos. Encourage highly focused images as opposed to landscapes or entire objects.

Once everyone has completed this assignment, the teams should come together and pick the best photo from each team member. This will cause much discussion and differing opinions. Team members email the chosen photos to the instructor, who will organize a slideshow for the following class period. During the slide show, all images can be shown to the class (set to music to make it more interesting) the first time through the slideshow. Play the slideshow a second time, stopping at each image and allowing students to identify their image and provide a brief explanation as to why they chose that image. The instructor should determine the appropriate age for this challenge; we recommend this challenge for middle school and high school students.

Equipment

- A camera for each student (preferably the camera on a personal smartphone; if a student does not have a camera, the team must share the cameras they have)

Setup

The instructor should gather the teams together in an activity area. If possible, take the students to a park or forest close to the school. Once gathered, the instructor gives each team 20 to 30 minutes to venture forth as a team. Team members stay fairly close together, but each teammate looks separately for something he or she would like to photograph. Once each teammate has taken three pictures, the team should come together and make some photo decisions.

Rules and Sacrifices

1. This is an individual activity as well as a team activity. Students should be informed that they will be sharing their image and be prepared to discuss why they chose it.
2. Images are encouraged to be of natural origin, but manmade objects can be considered as well.

Possible Solutions

Everyone must have the use of a camera; if some teammates do not have a camera, those who do must share. The team must use their imaginations to take the most creative pictures possible and then send them to the teacher.

Conclusion of the Task

When the instructor has been sent all the pictures that were taken by the students, the task is over.

Additions and Variations

- Instead of sending images to the instructor for private sharing with the class, students could also post their photos, and corresponding responses if desired, to their social media pages on Facebook or Instagram. This allows a higher degree of exposure and ownership of the activity.
- Let each team print their photos and then collaborate to make a large collage using tagboard and tape. Post their work in the school hallway.
- To make this a real team challenge, the team could decide on one picture out of all the pictures taken by the team to send to the instructor.

METEOR SHOWER

This challenge was first published in *40 Years in the Gym*. Teams meet the challenge when the rocket launcher propels the astronaut through space to the finish line in one push and the astronaut catches all five meteors (tennis balls) during flight. Use this challenge only after you have provided instructions on scooter safety and appropriate throws.

Equipment

- Five tennis balls
- Five bases or poly spots
- One scooter

Setup

Mark an area of the gym 30 to 40 feet (9 to 12 meters) for space travel. An astronaut sits on a scooter at one end of space (activity area), and a rocket launcher (teammate who pushes him or her) stands behind the astronaut. Both are behind the starting line. Five team members line up on bases or poly spots along one side of the playing area (see diagram). These teammates face the playing area, and each throws a tennis ball to the astronaut as he or she flies through space.

You can make the playing area longer if you need to accommodate more team members.

Rules and Sacrifices

1. The rocket launcher must remain behind the starting line.
2. The astronaut must not touch the floor with any body part, and the scooter must remain three-fourths of the width of the area (15 feet [4.5 meters])

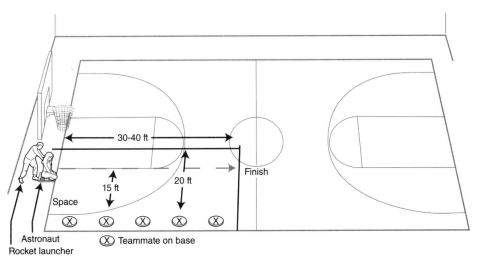

Setup for Meteor Shower.

away from the throwers. You can use cones to show where the boundary is or just estimate.

3. The astronaut must catch the balls with his or her hands.

4. If the astronaut fails to catch all five meteors or any of the other rules are broken, players rotate and attempt the challenge again. The rocket launcher becomes the new astronaut, and the astronaut goes to the last base. Each teammate on a base moves one base closer to the starting line. The base closest to the start becomes the new rocket launcher.

5. The astronaut must travel to the finish line with just one push. If he or she doesn't reach the finish line, the team must try again, even if the astronaut has caught all the meteors.

6. Group members cannot use last names or put-downs.

Possible Solutions

This is a fairly difficult challenge; however, with some practice, every team will eventually be able to solve it. The rocket launcher cannot push the astronaut too hard or the astronaut will not have time to catch the balls because he or she will be moving too fast. An easy underhand toss by the teammates on the bases is the best way to deliver the ball. Each tosser must toss after the astronaut has successfully caught and tucked away the previous ball.

Conclusion of the Task

The task is concluded when the astronaut arrives back to Earth in one push and has successfully caught all of the meteors.

Additions and Variations

- Add barriers in space, such as cones, that the astronaut may not touch.
- Increase or decrease the number of balls.
- Make the challenge more or less difficult by using different equipment for the meteors (e.g., beanbags or yarn balls).
- Place throwers on both sides of the playing area.
- Alter the distance from the throwers to the astronaut.
- Use larger balls.

Safety Considerations

Discuss scooter safety. Please check that the rocket launchers push the astronaut from the shoulders. If they push the scooters, the astronaut could fall backwards. Be careful when throwing the ball to the astronaut. The astronaut must be aware the ball is coming.

BUILDING BLOCKS

Doug Hicks and Bobbie Bigwood provided this challenge. The team must build a vertical tower that is eight building blocks high. Each block must be stacked in a different manner. The instructor may decide to put a letter on each block so that a word will be spelled out vertically with the first letter on the highest block. The students have to figure out what the word is prior to building the tower.

Equipment
- Eight 15-inch (38-centimeter) cardboard boxes (building blocks)

Setup
All the blocks are lying randomly on the floor. The team members gather around the building blocks to discuss their strategy. They need to figure out the word that is printed on the boxes.

Rules and Sacrifices
1. If the tower falls, the group must start over.
2. Two people must stack a block together using agreed-upon body parts. The block must be picked up by both team members.
3. The next block must be stacked by two different partners using a combination of two different body parts. Each block must be stacked by a new combination of partners using two new body parts. For example, if both partners use their hands to stack a block, hands with hands cannot be used again; one partner using hands and one using elbows could be used.
4. The tower must spell out a word with the first letter of the word on the top box.
5. Group members cannot use last names or put-downs.
6. If any rule is broken, the tower must be rebuilt.

Possible Solutions
Team members may try to throw blocks to the top of the tower. This difficult method will likely result in failure. Success will more likely come from building a few smaller towers and then adding these on top of one another.

Group members will need to figure out the best ways to lift the blocks as the challenge develops. If two partners lift the first block using both hands, no one will be able to use two hands again for the rest of the task. Therefore, saving this method for the very last move would be a good strategy. The best solution may be to make two stacks of four blocks each and then lift one stack using both hands of two partners onto another stack of four boxes.

Conclusion of the Task

When all eight boxes are stacked vertically and the word is spelled correctly, the task is complete.

Additions and Variations

- Blindfold half of the team. Only the blindfolded members may stack a block. Blindfold members may not speak. Sighted team members may not touch a block but must give concise directions to the two blindfolded teammates attempting to stack a box.
- Put an eight-letter character education word on the boxes, with one letter on each box, such as *kindness* or *courtesy*. Require the team to give a definition of the word before completing the challenge.

Safety Considerations

Do not allow the students to get on one another's shoulders to place the last box. Be careful of the tower falling, and do not push the tower over when the challenge is over; dismantle it carefully. If you use the blindfold variation, do not let the blind students wander around. They should stay seated until given directions.

RAINBOW SWAMP TRAIL

This challenge uses minimal equipment but requires constant communication and physical support as the group attempts to solve the task.

Each member of the team must get to the other side of the swamp. Along the way, each team member must retrieve a beanbag with a character education word and definition on it and take it with him or her to dry land. The group must plan a route through the bog on the stepping stones. Some of the stepping stones are slippery and can only hold one teammate. Students must be careful so that they don't fall into the swamp!

Equipment

- One dozen 12-inch (30-centimeter) poly spots (or bases)
- Six character education rainbow beanbags (beanbags of different colors), available through Gopher Sport (if commercially made beanbags are not available, then write a character education word on the bags)

Setup

Designate a starting line and a finish line. The swamp is the area between the two lines, which should be about 15 feet (4.5 meters) apart. Place the poly spots in a parallel line between the starting line and the finish line.

The poly spots (stepping stones) should be about one giant step apart. The distance varies with the age of your students, from up to 4 feet (120 centimeters) apart for middle school and down to 18 inches (45 centimeters) for first graders. Place the six beanbags near poly spots 2, 3, 5, 7, 9, and 10. The beanbags should be 2 to 4 feet (60 to 120 centimeters) away from the poly spots, depending on the age and size of your students. A person 5 feet (150 centimeters) tall can reach a beanbag 4 feet (120 centimeters) away without stepping off the spot but needs a lot of support to reach it. Here is a suggested list of distances for a group of sixth graders:

- Place a yellow character education beanbag 3 feet (90 centimeters) away from poly spot 2.
- Place a red character education beanbag 2 feet (60 centimeters) away from poly spot 3.
- Place a green character education beanbag 4 feet (120 centimeters) away from poly spot 5.
- Place an orange character education beanbag 3.5 feet (105 centimeters) away from poly spot 7.
- Place a blue character education beanbag 2 feet (60 centimeters) away from poly spot 9.
- Place a purple character education beanbag 4 feet (120 centimeters) away from poly spot 10.

Rules and Sacrifices

1. The team must hold hands and stay connected throughout its trip through the swamp. A team member who is attempting to pick up a beanbag may let go of one other teammate's hand but must rejoin hands before moving to another base.

2. No one may touch the floor during the trip through the swamp. If a team member breaks either rule 1 or rule 2, the group must start the task from the beginning.

3. Each team member must collect one beanbag on the journey and take it across the swamp. The beanbag cannot be dropped. If it is dropped, the beanbag must be replaced in its original position and retrieved again.

4. Team members must read the character education word and give the definition after they retrieve the bag.

5. Group members cannot use last names or put-downs.

Possible Solutions

The team must discuss which team member should get which beanbag. The taller teammates should get the beanbags that are the farthest away. The team also has to figure out how best to assist students who cannot easily reach their beanbags. Team members must move slowly and communicate constantly to avoid pulling a teammate off a stepping stone.

Conclusion of the Task

The team completes the task when all team members and all beanbags are on the shore beyond the finish line.

Additions and Variations

- Make one base a slippery base. Only one foot at a time is allowed to touch this base.
- Require the team to be silent except for one person who directs the team.
- Time the team to set a course record.
- To increase difficulty, set up bases in two lines rather than one; this option is shown in the video on the web resource.

Safety Considerations

Place the poly spots or bases with tape backing so that they do not slide. If group members begin to fall and do not let go of one another's hands, many people could lose their balance. The group should discuss the difference between trying to hold someone up and allowing the group to break apart so that the whole group does not fall.

Don't let anyone fall in the swamp!

CHARACTER CONNECTION CHALLENGE

This challenge was written for the outdoors, but it could be done in the gym as well. If done inside, the materials could be beanbags, soft balls, foam noodles, etc. Each team picks a character education word out of a bag. Each team should select one person to draw a word from the bag. Teams must spell out their chosen word with their bodies and items from nature. The teams can use grass, leaves, sticks, rocks, hay, sand, etc. One team member is chosen as the builder and directs or assists the team in creating its word. No team members other than the builder can speak. The builder is not a part of the word but notifies the instructor when the word is complete. The instructor should not know what word the team is spelling but must be able to read the word when the team is done. If the instructor cannot understand the word, he or she should walk away and come back in five minutes; this will give the team another chance to make its word more legible.

Equipment

- Building materials found in nature or provided in the gym

Setup

This is an indoor or outdoor challenge. Each team draws a character education word, such as *pride, respect, loyalty, tolerance, honesty, kindness, diligence,* or *initiative,* out of a bag. The instructor should not see the word each team draws. Teams try to create that word using the following rules.

Rules and Sacrifices

1. One team member should be selected to draw the word out of the bag. Do not let the teacher see the word.
2. One team member is selected to be the builder. Only the builder may speak during the building of the word.
3. The team must collect items from nature to help construct its word. The word cannot be built by team members' bodies only; it must also contain at least two different items from nature.
4. The builder may not touch any teammate.
5. The builder calls for the instructor when the word is done. If the instructor understands the word, the team has successfully completed the challenge.
6. If any rule is broken, the group must wait five minutes before starting construction again. If the teacher cannot identify the word, the group has five minutes to make the word more legible.

Possible Solutions

Students must decide how to use the items from nature, or the materials provided in the gym, along with their bodies, to complete the word chosen from the bag.

Conclusion of the Task

The challenge is completed when the word chosen from the bag is successfully spelled using their bodies and materials provided.

Additions and Variations

- Specify how many team members can lie down, sit, or stand. For instance, only five team members can be lying down when the word is finished. The rest of the team must be sitting, standing, or kneeling.
- Start with character words such as *caring, honesty,* or *pride* then move to larger words such as *perseverance* or *diligence.*
- Construct the word using at least three items from nature.
- Allow the team members to use any items they find, even if they are not found in nature (such as a bike or a playground log).
- Allow all team members to speak.
- Time the activity.
- Take a picture of each word to post in the gym.

Safety Considerations

Use with caution items from nature such as rocks or sticks. If students are allowed to gather items from nature, check that there are no poisonous plants around. Remind students not to pick flowers or plants when gathering items from nature.

LEAN ON ME

Lean on Me is a unique challenge developed for a large group and is a great culminating challenge for the team-building unit. We have had groups as large as 36 complete this task. The group holds on to a rope that is formed into a circle (tie the ends of the rope together). The rope can be from 70 to 100 feet (21 to 30 meters) long. The length of the rope depends on the size and number of students. We recommend a 100-foot (30-meter) rope for 25 sophomores. The group lets go of the rope by twos until the fewest number of remaining people can keep the rope off the ground without moving their feet or bending their elbows.

Group members space themselves evenly around the rope then step backward until the rope is taut. Every group member holds on to the rope with two hands with their elbows straight. Each group member has memorized a character education word or a character education definition. Group members have to decide which two people should let go of the rope and when they should release it. Only group members with a matching character word and definition may let go of the rope. For instance, a student with a character education word may not let go until the group comes up with the correct matching definition. After the team member with the matching definition reads it, the paired group members may let go of the rope. The group continues to release matching pairs until the remaining group members can no longer support the rope, the rope touches the ground, or someone moves his or her feet.

Equipment

- A very long rope, such as a tug-of-war rope or a long sash cord rope (tie the ends together to make a circle)
- One vinyl base or poly spot per person
- Character education word and definition cards should be given to the students prior to the challenge for memorization

Setup

You need a large, open area, indoors or outdoors, in which to conduct this challenge. After group members hold on to the rope with their arms extended, give each person a base on which to stand. Students cannot move off these bases until they have released the rope with their hands. You should have an equal number of words and matching definitions.

Rules and Sacrifices

1. Group members may not step off a base until they have released the rope with their hands.
2. Group members may not move their hands on the rope once they have started the task.
3. Group members must not bend their elbows while holding the rope.

4. The team must match a character education word and the definition before the team members with that word and definition can release the rope and step off the base. One set of team members steps off at a time.

5. Group members cannot use last names or put-downs.

6. The rope can never touch the ground.

7. Once students let go of the rope, they may not touch it again, but they may touch other students that are still holding the rope. This is to keep the rope from touching the ground. In addition, students will need to help each other balance on their bases as parts of the rope are let go of.

Possible Solutions

Prior to the activity, the team should study the focus words and their definitions. The students with matching words and definitions should be opposite one another in the circle so it will not cause the rope to touch the ground when they let go of the rope. Once two students have let go of the rope, they should help those who are still holding the rope to balance.

Conclusion of the Task

The challenge attempt is over when the rope hits the floor, when someone bends his or her elbows, when someone steps off a base before releasing the rope, or when the group feels that it has reached its limit. You may want to set a predetermined number of attempts for this challenge before starting the task.

Additions and Variations

- Experiment with different numbers of participants.

Safety Considerations

As with other challenges that use poly spots or vinyl bases, you should make sure that they stick to the floor so that participants cannot slip from their positions. Falling is a possibility if a group member loses his or her balance and cannot regain it.

Beanbag Boogie

This concept was invented by students at one of our many team-building classes. It is not a particularly physical challenge but will require a lot of communication and teamwork.

Equipment

- One large ball, such as a cage ball or yoga ball (the ball should be bigger than a basketball)
- Six 8-foot (2.5-meter) cloth jump ropes
- Twenty poly spots
- Ten beanbags

Setup

This challenge can be done in one half of the gym. Place the tire or hoop in the center of the court. Evenly distribute the poly spots inside the court. Evenly distribute the beanbags inside the court. Place the large ball on top of the tire or inside the hula hoop. Lay the six cloth ropes alongside the ball.

Rules and Sacrifices

1. The poly spots are hazards and cannot be touched by any team member.
2. The ball cannot be touched by the arms or hands of any team member.
3. The ball can never touch the ground.
4. The ball must be suspended by the ropes and must stay suspended during the collection of the beanbags.
5. The ball must be replaced on the tire or in the hoop after all beanbags have been collected. The ball is safe on the tire or in the hoop.
6. Group members cannot use last names or put-downs.
7. Beanbags must be collected and placed in the tire or hoop one at a time, and every team member must collect at least one beanbag.
8. If any rule is broken, all beanbags that have successfully been collected must be returned to the inside of the court and the team must start over.

Possible Solutions

This challenge requires a lot of communication. The group must decide how to suspend the ball on the ropes. The team should determine the order in which the beanbags should be picked up and placed in the hoop.

Conclusion of the Task

The challenge will be complete when all beanbags have been collected and are placed on the tire or in the hoop. The group must collect the beanbags while suspending the ball in the air and then return the ball to the tire or hoop when the beanbags have been collected. No poly spots can be touched during this effort.

Additions and Variations

- Add more beanbags.
- Place additional cones that students would need to go around.
- Increase or decrease the size of the area with which the challenge can be done.
- Use your imagination to make this challenge more creative.

Safety Considerations

This challenge does not present obvious safety considerations.

Chapter 8

Advanced Challenges

The challenges found in this chapter are physically or intellectually more difficult than the introductory and intermediate challenges. Instructors rarely give advanced challenges to students below sixth grade. We start every age group with introductory challenges. The younger the age group, the longer we stay with the introductory challenges. We move to intermediate and advanced challenges after teams show that they can accomplish the introductory challenges. The preparedness of the group, the instructor's trust in the group, and the demonstrated maturity level of the group are greater indicators than age when determining a group's readiness for an advanced challenge. Nevertheless, the older the group, the sooner we move to the advanced challenges because the introductory challenges are easier for older students.

The advanced challenges require more planning, physical assistance, and encouragement from all team members than the introductory and intermediate challenges. The advanced challenges teach students to persevere after failure. All advanced challenges can be modified to allow even young children to attempt them. Youngsters in the primary grades probably could not complete the Black Hole, but they could do any of the other challenges if modified appropriately.

BLACK HOLE

VIDEO ▶

Black Hole is both physically and intellectually challenging. In addition, team members must cooperate and trust each other. Group members try to pass through a hula hoop suspended from a basketball hoop. Students cannot touch the hoop (known as the black hole) nor can they dive through it. Group members must help each other and offer lots of physical support during the challenge. If group members have not worked together before, they may not have developed sufficient team-building skills to master this challenge.

Group members begin on one side of the hula hoop and must remain on the tumbling mats during the challenge. To pass through the hoop to the other side, group members need help from teammates.

Equipment

- Two tires
- One hula hoop
- A rope and masking tape to suspend the hoop between the tires and the basket
- At least four tumbling mats (see diagram)
- Mats or crash pads at least 4 inches thick

Setup

Suspend the hula hoop between the tires so that the bottom of the hoop is approximately 3 feet (1 meter) off the floor. You may need to modify the height of the hoop to accommodate shorter students; set the hoop height so that the bottom is about waist-high on most of the students.

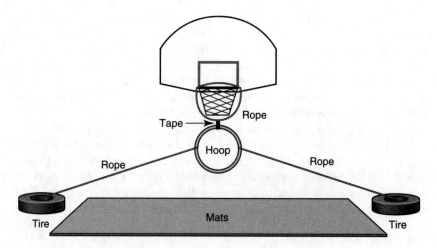

Black Hole equipment and setup.

Next, place at least four tumbling mats in the work space with at least two on each side of the hoop. Place the crash pad on the exit side of the hula hoop. Use a tape line to divide the work area into two distinct spaces, much like the center line of a volleyball court. Provide enough cushion in the work space so that a group member who falls will be well protected.

Rules and Sacrifices

1. All group members must go through the black hole (hoop).
2. No person may touch the black hole or the ropes connected to the hoop.
3. No one may step over the dividing line.
4. No one may dive through the hoop.
5. Group members may not reach under, around, or over the hula hoop to help. They may reach through the hoop to help.
6. Group members must remain on the tumbling mats during the challenge.
7. Group members cannot use last names or put-downs.
8. If a group member breaks a rule, that person and a teammate who has passed through the hoop must start again.

Getting the last person through the hoop is the hardest part of the challenge.

Possible Solutions

Most groups start by lifting and sliding one group member through the hoop while keeping his or her body straight. After the first person passes through the hoop, group members will be on both sides of the black hole to help their teammates through the hoop. Getting the last person through the hoop presents the greatest difficulty. Teammates on the Earth side of the black hole may reach across to the outer-space side as long as they do not touch the hoop or the floor on the outer-space side.

Conclusion of the Task

At the conclusion of the task, all group members stand on the Earth side of the black hole and remain on the mats until receiving approval from the instructor.

Additions and Variations

- You can lower the height of the hoop for younger children and raise it for more mature groups.
- Assigning group members to bring back moon souvenirs adds difficulty and interest to the task. Group members carry various objects (a football, basketball, beach ball, floor hockey stick, or other item) with them to Earth. The object must remain in contact with the person carrying it. Students cannot simply pass the items to one another through the hoop.
- Establish a time limit (15 or 20 minutes) for the challenge. Develop descriptive story lines to enhance the task for younger groups ("Darth Vader will be here in 15 minutes . . .").

This challenge involves trust and cooperation, and it is an excellent progression from intermediate challenges to demonstrate that help from teammates is necessary for success.

Safety Considerations

Use enough mats so that the work space is well cushioned and safe. Group members must lift and move each other carefully. If group members fall on the hoop, the hoop could break (but better to lose a hoop than have a student injured). Under no circumstances should you allow participants to dive through the hoop or throw a teammate through the black hole. Before the task begins, discuss the fact that teammates are putting their trust in the group. Group members must do everything they can to keep teammates supported (physically) when helping them move. Make certain that the floor area is well covered with mats and crash pads. When attaching the hoop to an overhead rope, attach the hoop to the rope with a piece of masking tape. That way, if someone falls onto the hoop, the tape will immediately snap, and the person passing through the hoop will not be caught on the hanging hoop.

STEPPING STONES II

Stepping Stones II is a real brain buster that requires much thinking and communication. This challenge, the most difficult thinking task in the book, does not require the group to work hard physically; it is more like a human chess game. Cooperation and planning are essential to solving the task.

Use this challenge after students have completed several other challenges or assign it to groups that demonstrate exceptional team-building skills. Refer to Additions and Variations for ideas on simplifying this challenge for younger students and others.

In this challenge, the group tries to rearrange itself from a specific starting order to a specific ending order. Group members stand in a straight line on bases, which they cannot move. The team divides itself into two equal groups, and the groups face each other. Having an even number of participants is helpful but not necessary.

Example: Eight students using nine bases.

Starting order:

A	B	C	D	empty base	1	2	3	4

Ending Order:

1	2	3	4	empty base	A	B	C	D

Cooperation and planning are essential for solving this task.

Equipment

- One base per group member
- One extra base

Setup

A space 5 to 8 feet (1.5 to 2.5 meters) wide and about 20 feet (6 meters) long is adequate. Place the bases in a straight line about 18 inches (45 centimeters) apart. One group member stands on each base, and the empty base is in the middle of the line.

The team divides into two groups. Each teammate receives a letter or number to designate his or her starting position. Alternatively, provide colored jerseys so that group members can identify their sections.

Rules and Sacrifices

1. Each group member must remain on a base except when moving to another base.
2. A person may only move forward to another base.
3. Only one person at a time may occupy a base.
4. When moving to a new base, a group member may move forward one base or around one teammate to another base, but team members may not move around two teammates in one move.
5. Only one group member at a time may move.
6. If a group member breaks a rule or if a group cannot make another move, the group must go back to its starting order.
7. Group members cannot use last names or put-downs.

Possible Solutions

The solution to this challenge is so specific that you might want to practice it by making your own board game. Draw nine squares on construction paper, place numbers and letters on eight checkers or domino pieces (see diagram), and practice these moves:

Step 1—D moves forward to empty base.

Step 2—1 moves around D to empty base.

Step 3—2 moves forward to empty base.

Step 4—D moves around 2 to open base.

Step 5—C moves around 1.

Step 6—B moves forward to open base.

Step 7—1 moves around B.

Step 8—2 moves around C.

Step 9—3 moves around D.

Step 10—4 moves forward to open base.

Step 11—D moves around 4 (D finishes).

Step 12—C moves around 3.

Step 13—B moves around 2.

Step 14—A moves around 1.

Step 15—1 moves forward (1 finishes).

Step 16—2 moves around A (2 finishes).

Step 17—3 moves around B.

Step 18—4 moves around C.

Step 19—C moves forward (C finishes).

Step 20—B moves around 4 (B finishes).

Step 21—A moves around 3.

Step 22—3 moves forward (3 finishes).

Step 23—4 moves around A (4 finishes).

Step 24—A moves forward (the task is complete).

See why we called it a human chess game? Group members need to constantly communicate with one another.

Solving the Stepping Stones II challenge.

Conclusion of the Task

The group masters the challenge when group members have moved from their beginning order to the designated ending order. To prevent frustration, group members may need to practice the challenge as a board game before trying it as a physical challenge.

Additions and Variations

- Have group members start by practicing in a four-person group (this task takes eight moves) or in a six-person group (this task takes 15 moves).
- To give your group visual help, tape a letter or number to each member's jersey. One group could wear red jerseys with the letters A, B, C, and D. The other group could wear blue jerseys with the numbers 1, 2, 3, and 4.

This difficult challenge is not suitable for groups that had trouble with easier tasks. Make modifications that we have overlooked. Keep in mind that this challenge requires more mental gymnastics and communication skills than it does physical skills. Groups that master this challenge should be considered proficient, cooperative problem solvers.

Safety Considerations

This challenge presents no apparent safety considerations.

ALPHABET BALANCE BEAM

Alphabet Balance Beam requires group members to help each other as they alphabetize themselves while remaining on top of a high balance beam.

Students cannot touch the floor or the supporting legs of the balance beam during this challenge.

Group members try to rearrange themselves alphabetically. They begin by sitting in random order on the beam. Give numbers to group members to help them remember the starting order. Before students read their instructions (the challenge card), specify the following information:

1. The name that the group will use for the alphabetical order, such as first name, middle name, last name, mother's first name, or father's first name

2. Whether students will alphabetize themselves from right to left or left to right

Equipment
- A high balance beam
- 8 to 10 tumbling mats
- At least two crash pads
- Enough tumbling mats to cover the entire work area

Setup
Choose a space away from walls or other equipment. Place two unfolded mats on the floor, end to end, and set the balance beam on the mats. Place one or two tumbling mats between the support legs of the beam to cover any leg extensions

The challenge begins with group members sitting in random order on the beam.

that touch the floor. Use more mats to cover the outside of the legs. Place mats or crash pads behind where the group will stand on the beam. Make sure that the work area is safe.

As students begin, they need to discuss which name (first, middle, last, or other) they will use in the task. You may need to help some students spell certain names. Students need to communicate how they need help and how they can help others.

Rules and Sacrifices

1. All group members must remain on the beam during the task.
2. If anyone touches a mat, the floor, or the legs of the beam, the entire group must get off the beam and start over.
3. Group members cannot use last names (unless last names were chosen for the task) or put-downs.

Possible Solutions

In solving this challenge, group members often hold tightly to the balance beam while a teammate steps carefully over them. Some students try to change positions while everyone is standing, and some students may maneuver under the beam. Some group members will probably lose their balance, so group members must guard against a fall. No one should be deliberately careless.

This task is easier when group members help each other. Some will need additional support just to maintain their balance while sitting.

Conclusion of the Task

The group completes the task when its members are standing on the beam in the correct order. Standing up on the beam may be harder than alphabetizing. Students

This task is easier when group members help each other.

need to plan how to stand and how to support each other. Don't be surprised to see a group make errors at this stage.

When the entire group is standing, have the group recite the names it used to achieve alphabetical order. Have group members recheck their alphabetized names before they stand.

Additions and Variations

- You may need to experiment to find the height at which to set the beam so that students cannot touch the mats with their feet while sitting on the balance beam.
- When assigning the order, make sure that the group members are not already seated alphabetically.
- Vary the direction of order often so that students can't anticipate the upcoming task. If a group has to change only a few places to achieve success, the task becomes less challenging and less fun.

Safety Considerations

As with many challenges, you must make sure that mats cover all of the work area. Additionally, cover any metal base parts of the beam with mats. Check the beam for any possibility of splintered wood. Have crash pads behind and in front of the beam to protect participants from dangerous falls.

Find out whether any participants have a fear of heights. Standing on the beam may be a fearful prospect for some people. Be sure to use a beam that can support the weight of the participants.

KNIGHTS OF THE AROUND TABLE

Team building has given us the opportunity to meet with many teachers. These meetings often evolve into a lively exchange of team-building ideas. Knights of the Around Table, a difficult and unique challenge, was created during one of these workshops. This challenge is a good lead-up to Electric Fence later in this chapter.

The group stands behind the starting line, which runs the length of a sturdy table and is positioned 3 feet (1 meter) from the side of the table. The group must transfer all members over, under, and then over the table again, without touching the floor. All group members must exit the top of the table beyond the finish line, which runs the length of the table opposite the starting line. The finish line should also be 3 feet (1 meter) from the table (see diagram).

Equipment

- A sturdy table (not a folding table as it may collapse)
- A roll of tape
- Two large folding mats

Setup

Place the mats side by side. Set the table on top of the mats. Make sure that the table is not wobbly and that all the table legs are secure. Use tape to create a starting line that runs the length of the table and is 3 feet (1 meter) from the side of the table. Create a finish line on the opposite side of the table from the starting line.

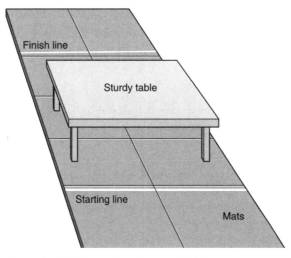

Setup for Knights of the Around Table.

Rules and Sacrifices

1. Group members may not touch the floor between the starting line and finish line.
2. Group members standing behind either tape line may assist a team member get on or around the table but may not touch the table (or allow three people to touch the table at the instructor's discretion).
3. After a group member gets off the table and crosses the finish line, he or she may not get back on top of the table.
4. Group members cannot use last names or put-downs.
5. If a group member breaks a rule, that person and one successful person (or the person who has advanced the farthest) must start the task again.

Possible Solutions

A team will succeed in this challenge only if it has a strategy to provide physical assistance to all team members. Team members should select the most athletic person to go first, and the team should assist that person from behind the starting line. After the first person travels under the table and successfully reaches the top, he or she should stay on top of the table to assist others. Another strategy is to send two people to the top of the table before anyone attempts to crawl under and over.

Getting someone to the finish line and allowing him or her to help from that position is helpful. Remember, providing physical assistance from behind the starting and finish lines is permitted as long as those assisting do not touch the table.

Conclusion of the Task

The group masters the task when all group members have traveled over, under, and then over the table again and are standing behind the finish line.

Additions and Variations

- Use a wider table for older students and a narrower table for younger students.
- Adjust the distance of the starting and finish lines.
- Have the team attempt to transport a football dummy (injury victim) over, under, and then over the table.
- Put a time limit on the journey.
- Allow a certain number of students that are behind the starting or finish line to touch the table while assisting.

Safety Considerations

Because teammates will be leaning and hanging over, under, and around a table, the likelihood of getting bruises is significant. Participants can lose their grip and fall, especially while hanging under the table. Teammates need to be careful when helping a group member. If they hang on to a teammate too tightly or carelessly, they could cause a fall or pull muscles. Group members attempting to go under the table should not go feetfirst because they could slip, lose their grip, and land on their backs or hit their heads on the tumbling mats. Make sure that the table does not have any sharp edges or splintered surfaces that could cause a cut or splinter.

Electric Fence

Students of all ages enjoy Electric Fence, and it can be easily modified for most students. This task requires a group to progress from one end of a high balance beam to the other end. The catch is that group members must go under a net (electric fence) hanging perpendicularly above and touching the beam—but the students can't touch the net. Even in modified form, this challenge is one of the more physically demanding tasks in the book.

All group members must crawl, slide, or hang like monkeys as they move from an entry mat (at one end of the beam) to an exit mat (at the other end). The group also must cross under the electric fence (a net hanging above the beam).

Equipment

- A high balance beam
- At least seven tumbling mats
- A badminton or volleyball net
- Two badminton or volleyball net standards

Setup

Place two mats end to end on the floor and set the balance beam on them. The beam should be high enough that the tallest student cannot touch the floor when hanging under the beam. Put additional mats under the beam to cover its legs and their extensions. Next, set a folded tumbling mat perpendicular to the beam at each end of the beam. These mats, which may also be called the ledges, serve as entry and exit mats. Place the net so that it bisects the beam. The net should hang from the standards so that it brushes the top of the beam. Cover all floor space beneath the work area with tumbling mats.

To complete this challenge, students hang under the beam and move like monkeys. Group members on the entry mat (ledge 1) support a guider who could sit either on or below the beam. The purpose of the guider is to provide assistance to the team member who is hanging below the beam and attempting to get back on top. Group members on the exit mat (ledge 2) help a guider on the other side of the beam. This challenge is difficult, and the group may need several attempts to succeed.

Rules and Sacrifices

1. The students must begin the task by getting on top of the balance beam.
2. The students may not touch the floor or tumbling mats between the entry and exit mats (ledges 1 and 2).
3. Group members must go under the net without touching it.
4. The students must get back on the top of the beam before getting off the beam.
5. After a student gets off the beam and onto the exit mat, he or she may not get back onto the beam.

To complete this challenge, students hang under the beam and move like monkeys.

6. Only group members on the beam may help those hanging under the beam.

7. Group members must be on the ledge to help a teammate on top of the beam. Students on the ledge may not assist a student hanging under the beam.

8. If a group member breaks a rule, that person and a teammate who has crossed the beam must start over.

9. Group members cannot use last names or put-downs.

Possible Solutions

Students climb onto the beam one at a time; turn upside down, monkey style; and try to move along the beam and under the net. While a group member tries to go under the beam and under the net, group members on both sides of the net should offer help. Most students need help getting their feet under the electric fence and getting back on top of the beam. Group members need to decide when to get off the beam (refer to rule 5); if they get off the beam too soon, they may not be available to help their teammates. Constant encouragement and physical assistance are necessary during this challenge. Making a good choice of the first and last group members to travel the beam is also vital to solving the challenge.

Conclusion of the Task

To reach their goal, all group members must cross under the electric fence and stand on the exit mat (ledge 2).

Additions and Variations

- Place a tire on the floor (under the beam) for students to use as a support.
- Reduce the travel distance for younger students and then let them drop off carefully.
- Use a lightweight football dummy as an additional group member. The students can pretend that they are rescuing an injured group member.
- Assign a time limit. (Example: "A storm is coming. You have 20 minutes to complete the task.")

Safety Considerations

Make certain that tumbling mats cover the floor space. Cover any metal feet of the beam with mats. Suggest to participants that they wear long-sleeved shirts and long pants (such as sweatpants or running pants). This task can cause some bruises when participants attempt to get on top of the beam after hanging beneath it.

GRAND CANYON

Grand Canyon (previously known as Grand Canyon II) is an advanced challenge with complex teamwork required. Group members travel across an open space from one cliff to another using a climbing rope to swing across the Grand Canyon.

The group transfers its members from one cliff to another. They attempt to swing across the open space between the cliffs and land safely on the second cliff. Group members need to assist one another in both the swinging and landing process. The placement of the rope in relationship to the first cliff determines the difficulty of this challenge.

Equipment

- One climbing rope for swinging
- Two large crash pads for the two cliffs (or stack tumbling mats to create the two cliffs)
- Additional mats to place between the cliffs and over any floor space where the group may be working (when in doubt, mat the area)

Setup

Set the first cliff almost directly under the climbing rope, perhaps 1 to 2 feet (30 to 60 centimeters) away (see diagram). The closer the rope is to the cliff, the more difficult the challenge is. Locate the second cliff far enough away so that a person reaching it must stretch to make it onto that cliff. This distance will vary depending on your gym space and the length of the rope. Cover the floor area with tumbling mats. Place additional mats around the cliffs to reduce risk of injury should someone fall. If a cliff is near a wall, be sure to place crash pads against the wall so that students will not be hurt if they swing into the wall.

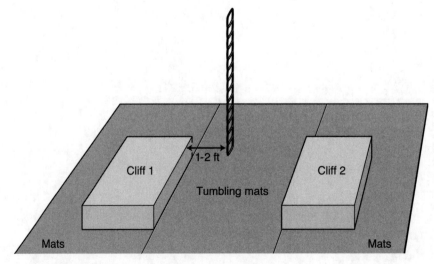

Grand Canyon setup.

Rules and Sacrifices

1. If a group member touches the floor (Grand Canyon), that person and one successful person must return to the first cliff.
2. If a group member falls off a cliff onto the floor, that person and one successful person must go back to the first cliff.
3. Group members cannot use last names or put-downs.

Possible Solutions

Although groups follow one basic pattern in solving this task, each group finds a unique challenge. The group begins by trying to find one person who can make it across the canyon and safely land on the second cliff. This process often takes a while. The group must find an efficient method to swing group members. Those who make it to the second cliff should help their teammates as they land. The group must also carefully choose the last person to swing across because that person will have to cross the canyon without the benefit of a push or other help. Balance is important because the group works off both cliffs. Carelessness will cause people to step off the cliffs, thus requiring the group to make a sacrifice. In addition, group members must make good choices in their sacrifices. If possible, they should not sacrifice people who were difficult to get across the canyon.

Conclusion of the Task

The group completes the challenge when all the group members have successfully made it across the canyon. They must all be standing on the second cliff (and they will be cheering wildly).

Additions and Variations

The placement of the first cliff and the distance to the second cliff determine the difficulty of this challenge. Make this task tough. The group should struggle. If you have a group member who needs a special adaptation, feel free to make an exception to the rules. A tire placed in the canyon could serve as a resting place or stepping stone. Do not allow the entire group to use the adaptation.

Safety Considerations

Participants need to take care while swinging on the rope. A person may possibly swing into a teammate. If a person jumps off the rope and lands poorly, he or she could twist an ankle or knee joint. Teammates who push people on the rope need to use good judgment and not swing the rope too hard or carelessly. They must not swing a teammate into a wall.

Spider's Web

Spider's Web can be done outside or indoors. You can make your own equipment or buy a commercially made frame with stretch (bungee) cords that snap in place to make the web design. The goal of this challenge is to get each team member through the spider's web without touching any part of it. An additional requirement is that each group member must pass through a different opening in the web.

The group begins on one side of the spider's web. The challenge is to get every group member through the web to the other side. Group members can help one another in a variety of ways. They must all pass through the web without touching it, and each must choose a different hole in the web to pass through. An exception is that a group member may use a space originally used by a teammate who had to start over because he or she broke a rule.

Equipment

- A commercially made spider's web (from Gopher Sport) or a web that you build using string, stretch cords, or sash cord material (the number of openings in the web should exceed the number of group members)
- Tumbling mats
- Small bells that ring if anyone touches the spider's web (optional)

Setup

Create the spider's web so that group members can pass through a number of openings and shapes as they attempt to move from one side of the web to the other. The openings should be large enough that participants have a reasonable chance of getting through the hole. Make sure that the support base is safe by using tumbling mats or crash pads or, for an outdoor web, be sure that the materials beneath the web are adequate to prevent anyone from getting hurt by a fall to the ground. Groups can do this challenge on a playground area that has pea gravel, wood chips, or deep sand as a safety base. Groups have also done the challenge outdoors in winter with a snow base.

Rules and Sacrifices

1. Each group member must pass through a different opening in the spider's web.
2. No one may touch any part of the web with his or her body.
3. Group members may reach through the web to help a teammate, but they may not touch the web.
4. No one may dive through an opening.
5. The group may not toss anyone through an opening.
6. Group members cannot use last names or put-downs.

Web openings should be large enough for team members to pass through.

© Gopher Sport

7. If a group member breaks a rule, that person and a successful teammate must start the task again.

8. If bells are hung from the spider's web, a sacrifice will be necessary if the bell makes a sound.

Possible Solutions

This challenge has a basic solution. Group members attempt to find the holes that are the easiest to pass through. Teammates should physically assist each other as they pass through the openings. As in the Black Hole challenge, no one may dive through the openings, and groups cannot toss anyone through. If the group lifts a group member off the ground to pass that person through an opening, those doing the lifting must make a commitment to that person's safety. If the spider's web is built outdoors or in a manner that would allow a group member to go under the web, you may wish to prohibit anyone from passing under the web or possibly allow only one person to use that path.

Conclusion of the Task

The group completes the challenge when all group members are on the opposite side of the spider's web from where they started.

Additions and Variations

We offer no additions or variations for this challenge.

Safety Considerations

As with the Black Hole challenge, do not allow participants to dive through openings. If group members plan to lift and pass teammates through openings in the spider's web, those doing the lifting need to make a safety commitment to the people they are lifting. The group may not throw a teammate through an opening, even if that person suggests the idea or volunteers to be thrown.

Neutral Zone

The Neutral Zone is one of the few advanced challenges created in one of our graduate team-building classes. Although the concept for solving this challenge is simple, the execution of the solution is difficult. The students who helped create this challenge built their own equipment, although the equipment is now commercially manufactured.

This challenge bears some similarities to the Stepping Stones challenges in that group members must change places during the task. The added level of difficulty occurs because group members balance on a teeter-totter device. The board on which the group balances may not touch the floor (or tumbling mats) while the group performs the challenge.

Equipment

- A balance board, balanced on a fulcrum, with numbered placements marked for group members and the middle marked as the neutral zone
- Tumbling mats throughout the work area

We made a balance board out of two 10-foot-long (3-meter-long) two-by-sixes. Place one two-by-six on top of the other and nail them together. Please look at the picture to get a better idea of the construction.

Note: The middle of the board sits between two raised edges on the fulcrum to keep it from swinging side to side. Examples can be found on YouTube by searching team balance board.

Setup

Place the balance board on tumbling mats and surround the entire work area with tumbling mats.

Rules and Sacrifices

1. No one may touch the ground (or mats) during the challenge.
2. The balance board may not touch the ground during the challenge.
3. Group members cannot use last names or put-downs.
4. Group members may step on the fulcrum when changing positions.
5. If the group breaks a rule, it must start the challenge from the beginning.

Possible Solutions

Teammates must constantly communicate and agree to all team movements. All movements should be done slowly and with assistance from teammates.

Conclusion of the Task

The group completes the challenge when its members are balanced on opposite sides of the balance board.

Teammates must move slowly and help each other.

Additions and Variations

- Have group members change places so that they line up in exact reverse order from their starting positions. For example, when starting in the order 4-3-2-1-1-2-3-4, team members must trade places with the same numbered person. This variation adds difficulty to the challenge and may not warrant the extra time needed to work through the sacrifices.
- Don't allow team members to step on the neutral-zone fulcrum.
- Allow a group a specified number of touches or errors (such as three) before it must make a sacrifice.

Safety Considerations

If a group member loses his or her balance in this challenge, he or she may try to hang on to a teammate and cause both to fall. If group members fall quickly or carelessly, the balance board and fulcrum could slip out of position. The group should be aware that fast or impulsive movements could cause the balance board to crash to the ground.

THINKING OUTSIDE THE DOTS

Thinking Outside the Dots was the result of our students taking a children's brainteaser activity and turning it into a team-building challenge. When used in a classroom setting, this activity requires the student to connect nine dots using four straight lines without lifting the pencil off the paper.

The group attempts to connect ropes in a straight-line manner so that the ropes pass over all nine poly spots set on the floor.

Equipment

- Nine poly spots or bases
- Four long jump ropes

Setup

Create a three-by-three patterned square with the bases approximately 6 feet (180 centimeters) apart. Lay the ropes on the floor to one side of the square.

Rules and Sacrifices

1. Team members may tie ropes together.
2. The team must suspend the ropes above the bases (dots) without touching the floor or bases during all attempts.

The team must connect all nine dots with no more than four rope segments.

3. The rope may pass over a base more than once, but no part of the rope may overlap.
4. If any part of the rope touches the floor, the attempt fails, and the team must begin the task again.
5. If the team creates more than four line segments, the attempt fails.
6. With each failed attempt, the team must start the task over with one fewer teammate being allowed to speak.
7. Group members cannot use last names or put-downs.

Possible Solutions

Although the common solution is similar to the paper-and-pencil solution, visualizing the solution while holding on to the ropes complicates the challenge. Keeping the ropes off the ground creates a much greater challenge than allowing the ropes to lie on the ground and poly spots.

Conclusion of the Task

The group is successful when it connects all nine dots with no more than four rope (line) segments. The ropes will be stretched in such a manner that they will go over (cover) each of the dots placed on the floor.

Additions and Variations

- To simplify the challenge, allow the ropes to lie on the ground and touch the bases.
- To make the challenge more difficult, spread the bases farther apart. You will need longer ropes for this variation.
- If a group gets completely stuck, give team members paper and pencils to help them discover the solution.

Safety Considerations

This challenge presents no apparent safety considerations.

Indiana's Challenge

Indiana's Challenge, created in one of our summer classes, has become one of our core challenges—not only because of its clever design but also because it doesn't require much space and uses very little equipment. In addition, the challenge has multiple solutions.

Group members gather around a 10-foot (3-meter) diameter circle, such as the jump ball circle of a basketball court. The challenge is to remove a basketball that is balanced on an 18-inch (45-centimeter) cone from the middle of the circle. Group members have jump ropes that they use to get the ball out of the circle. One element of the challenge is that the group must find three different ways to remove the ball. One of the three methods must include flinging the ball so that a group member can catch it in the air. Another element of the challenge is that the ball may not touch the floor either inside or outside the circle. In addition, no group member may step over the line or touch the inside of the circle with any body part. Whenever the ball falls to the floor, one group member may cross the line to place the ball back onto the cone. While in the circle, this group member may not help manipulate any of the ropes.

Equipment
- A basketball (or a volleyball for younger students)
- Four jump ropes, approximately 8 to 10 feet (2.6 to 3.0 meters) long (we recommend sash cord rope)

Setup
Place the 18-inch (45-centimeter) cone in the center of the 10-foot (3-meter) circle. Make sure that the cone has an opening that will allow a basketball to rest on the top of it. Place the ropes outside the circle. If you do not have an existing circle in your facility, create one with chalk or vinyl tape. You could use another shape, but a circle adds an interesting dimension when the group tries to move around.

Rules and Sacrifices
1. If the ball touches the floor, one group member may cross the circle line to replace the ball on the cone.
2. The teammate replacing the ball on the cone may not manipulate the ropes while in the circle.
3. Participants may not cross the line at any time while trying to remove the ball.
4. The ball may never touch the ground inside or outside of the circle.
5. Group members cannot use last names or put-downs.
6. If a group member breaks a rule, the group must stop, replace the ball, and begin again.

Possible Solutions

Almost every time we use this challenge, we see groups come up with new twists to solving it. One method is to cross the ropes so that two ropes are perpendicular to two other ropes. The group then creates a small cradle in which to rest the ball. Group members lift the ball and carry it out of the circle.

They also use this method to lift the ball and fling it into the air so that a group member can catch it. In both cases, group members must tightly hold the rope so that the ball does not slip through. Another method is to create a channel with the ropes. One side lifts its end of the ropes and rolls the ball to the other side of the circle, where a group member catches it. We have also seen a group place two ropes parallel to one another about 8 inches (20 centimeters) apart and then weave the other ropes back and forth to create a long, skinny net. The group uses this net to carry the ball out of the circle, roll the ball out of the circle, and fling the ball out of the circle.

Conclusion of the Task

The group completes the task when it creates three different methods of removing the ball from the cone. Group members should then replace the ball on the cone, untie any knots that they may have made, and place the equipment neatly outside the circle.

Additions and Variations

- If a team is successful with two different methods, challenge them with this statement: "For your third attempt, the ropes may not touch the ball." This will cause many quizzical looks, but the team will determine how to complete the challenge.

Teams can fling the ball in the air so someone can catch it.

Safety Considerations

Teams often loop the ropes around the waist of a teammate as that teammate leans forward and attempts to grab the ball off the cone; caution should be used so that the teammate does not tip forward and bang the floor. The team may want to hold that person's feet.

ABOUT THE AUTHORS

Courtesy of Leigh Anderson.

Leigh Anderson currently teaches in White Bear Lake, Minnesota, where she applies many of the concepts in this book. In addition to her elementary classroom and intervention experience, Leigh taught at the graduate level in the teaching and learning master's program at Saint Mary's University of Minnesota. This is the third book dealing with best practices in education that Leigh has coauthored, and she has presented both nationally and internationally. Leigh holds a bachelor's degree in elementary education and a master's degree in curriculum and instruction.

Daniel W. Midura is a former physical education specialist and coordinator in the Roseville Area School District in Roseville, Minnesota. Now retired, Midura was a physical education specialist for more than 40 years. In that time he has presented at more than 200 conferences and workshops and coauthored four books. He was named the Minnesota Physical Education Teacher of the Year in 1994 and was awarded the 1995 National Association for Sport and Physical Education (NASPE) Teacher of the Year for Minnesota, among other teaching awards and honors. He has served as president of the Minnesota Alliance for Health, Physical Education, Recreation and Dance (MNAHPERD), and he was an adjunct faculty member at Bethel University and Saint Mary's University of Minnesota.

Courtesy of Daniel W. Midura.

Courtesy of Donald R. Glover.

Donald R. Glover has taught physical education, including adapted physical education, since 1967 at the preschool, elementary, secondary, and postsecondary levels. He currently teaches adaptive physical education methods at the University of Wisconsin at River Falls.

In 1981, Glover was recognized as Minnesota's Teacher of the Year, and he was named the Minnesota Adapted Physical Education Teacher of the Year in 1989. He has written eight books, published numerous magazine and journal articles on physical education and sport, and been a clinician at more than 100 workshops and clinics.

Glover earned his master's degree in physical education from Winona State University in 1970. A former president of MNAHPERD, he is a member of SHAPE America and the Minnesota Education Association.